Downrange for the Duration

Kevin John Cullen

Cover and Interior Book Design by JuLee Brand for Kevin Anderson & Associates

Downrange For The Duration/ Kevin John Cullen. —1st ed.

ISBN 9781720284369

Contents

Downrange: (adj) In the direction of the intended flight path of a rocket or a missile; a term for being deployed overseas, usually in a war zone.

Foreword

The aftermath of the terrorist attacks on 9/11 prompted counterstrikes by US and coalition forces throughout Afghanistan. As the aggressive campaign to eradicate Al-Qaida and the Taliban expanded, so too did the mobilization of troops and the demand for operational support from civilian contractors.

Combat military forces are trained to live in austere conditions and manage the threats that exist on the battlefield. Handsome salary incentives were offered to augment the predominantly less qualified contractor workforce, who, in most cases, received little or no training before being deployed in harm's way. Most of the noncombatants, therefore, didn't know what to expect when they arrived in Afghanistan—but they figured it out rather quickly.

The emotional aftermath of 9/11 left much of America's population feeling devasted yet bitter. They wanted revenge upon those responsible for the murder of over three thousand US citizens. The US government's decision to spearhead the mobilization of an international coalition force was overwhelmingly supported but fighting an enemy that didn't have a formal army (or headquarters) proved rather daunting. Operation Desert Storm and the liberation of Kuwait lasted only one hundred hours before the Iraqi Army quit its campaign and returned home, defeated. Operation Enduring Freedom (the official name given to the war in Afghanistan by the US military) would last considerably longer.

By 2009 the ripple effect of America's Great Recession was negatively impacting the global economy. Americans weren't the only people struggling; countries who did business with America were hurting as well. As the saying goes, "Whenever America has a case of the sniffles, the rest of the world comes down with the flu."

Keeping the proverbial wolf away from the door—while providing support of a cause that endeavored to make the world safer—added a measure of comfort to thousands of civilians who were compelled to join the fight. Regardless of whatever reasons may have prompted them to serve, their courage for taking such bold steps was admirable.

Over 100,000 civilian contractors served in support of the war in Afghanistan. Most of the jobs were important but not terribly *sexy* in terms of making front-page headlines. As a construction supervisor overseeing military infrastructure projects, I never considered what I did as glamorous, not when compared to the jobs that required people to be exposed to constant risk. Driving a supply truck full of ammunition on the open highway (for example), subject to attacks from the Taliban, took nerves of steel. Many dangerous jobs were performed by average folks but whether you were a cook, a mechanic, or a construction worker, each and every job required a special level of skill and dedication. I smile whenever I think about the time when I served alongside some of the finest people I've ever met, in one of the worst places I've ever been.

The purpose behind writing this book was to elevate people's awareness about an average group of ordinary people who made extraordinary choices that led to significant contributions—both on and off the battlefield. My service in the Navy was a timely segue for my follow-on career choice as a contractor. From the day I left Afghanistan, armed with an M4 assault rifle and a nine-millimeter pistol, to the moment I returned, outfitted with my first pair of 5.11 tactical gear cargo pants and a color-coordinated Columbia shirt, less than six months had transpired. *Didn't I just leave this party?*

For me, the transition from combatant to noncombatant was seamless. The regional, cultural, and survival knowledge I obtained in the Navy provided me with the essential tools I needed to prosper as a contractor. Not everyone was as fortunate, however. Living and working in a war zone tended to complicate even the most attentive person's thought process. After years of being institutionalized within such a peculiar environment, perspectives tended to change and people's priorities were obscured by what had become a new reality.

Downrange for the Duration is a summary of my life before and during my tenure as a war zone contractor. Like many people who have spent time on the battlefield, the way I viewed things, including parts of my personal life— changed. I didn't see things the way I used to, and as a result, some adjustments were required after I returned home to the real world.

Writing about my experience in Afghanistan turned out to be both cathartic and educational; I rediscovered some things that were either lost in the fog of war or misplaced over time. My most sincere hope, therefore, is that others who had similar experiences—whether they (too) were war zone contractors or the spouses and/or dependents who felt as though they'd been left behind to fend for themselves, hopefully, they too will gain some insight and enjoyment from the pages ahead.

Without further ado therefore, and in the words of Todd Beamer, the heroic soul who on September 11, 2001, led his fellow passengers in overpowering the terrorists who had taken control of United Airlines Flight 93, words that civilian contractors oftentimes quoted as a reminder of what prompted us to join the fight in the global war on terror—*"Let's Roll."*

Kevin J. Cullen

Dedicated in memory of Steven Alexander Cullen.

CHAPTER 1

The Catalyst for Things to Come

My wife awoke with a start, pushed away the covers, and sprung out of bed. She hadn't heard the baby's cry and feared that she'd missed a feeding. Throwing on her robe, she moved quickly into the nursery, dragging an uncooperative slipper along the way. The sudden motion of the bed had awakened me, and as I opened my eyes I captured the faint image of her pink robe as she exited the bedroom. Groggy and unconcerned, I assumed that the baby was finally starting to sleep longer between feedings. *Hallelujah.*

The woman in the pink robe was my wife. I used the word *was* because we're not married anymore; something terrible happened and we grew apart. Before our son was born, we were going through some tough times. A downturn in the economy forced us to sell our house and the transition wasn't easy, especially on my wife, who at the time was pregnant with our son. The events that followed were life-changers, to say the least.

My wife, who I'll refer to as Sally (not her real name), was a proverbial stay-at-home mom who looked after the household while her husband went off to work each day. The fact that she stayed home was by design; we preferred the old-school arrangement so as to ensure a safe and proper upbringing for our children, which by last count had increased to three; our first two were a pair of darling little girls, affectionately nicknamed Peanut and Birdy, who, along with their newborn brother, were the loves of our lives.

Sally had her hands full each day, but she managed well, and I felt fortunate to have the support she provided. When I returned home from work, the smell of something delicious cooking for dinner hit me as I entered the front door. Both my wife and I preferred things to be tidy, so the house was always spotless. The kids' toys were never strewn about, the laundry had been folded and put away, and there were never any dishes piled up in the sink. Everything was shipshape, and to her credit Sally didn't have any help; she managed everything by herself and rarely complained.

Our newborn son was breastfed, and like his father he had a hearty appetite. We were convinced he had an alarm clock in his stomach that went off every two hours. The midnight feedings were taxing, but Sally, now a mother of three, was primed for the task. She was a veteran of two previous campaigns that yielded great victory, as evidenced by the health and happiness of our daughters. Sally rarely asked for my help because there was little for me to do with a newborn who was breastfed, save offer to change a diaper or hold the baby so she could have some time to herself—which I did. I love kids, especially my own.

Bedtime came early because everyone needed their rest. We bathed the girls after dinner, read them a story, and put them to bed. Shortly thereafter, Sally and I would retire as well. I got up early each morning in preparation for my ninety-minute commute to work. Sally, whose job was never done, was exhausted by eight o'clock in the evening. She hurried to bed so she could sleep a little before the baby woke up for his next turn at the filling station. Like most newborns, our little son woke up several times throughout the night, wet and hungry. He'd be wide awake at 2:00 a.m., while his parents were sleepwalking like a pair of zombies. Making matters worse, the little guy had a talent for purging his insides with a detonation that defied human potential. The force of his little butt-blast was like a gas explosion in the sewers that sent all the manhole covers along Main Street rocketing into the sky. The aftermath would produce a pungent puree that would cover his legs, find its way between his toes, and soak his little pajamas all the way up to the back up to his neck. The diaper changes were enough to knock out an elephant; tears would well up in my eyes, and my throat would burn. An adult suffering from the effects of severe food poisoning would be embarrassed by such an uncontrollable release—but not our kid; the look of excitement on his face seemed to suggest that he was proud of what he'd accomplished. If we were keeping score, we would have noted that he'd surpassed the previous night's record by not only soiling all of his clothes from head to toe, he had ruined yet another set of sheets and set off the smoke detector in his room.

As was customary, Sally was awakened by the baby's cries. She stumbled out of bed and headed to the nursery, down the hall. Having been awakened as well, I'd lie still in bed, listening to the familiar sounds coming from the baby monitor: the sound of the tape being pulled off his plastic diaper, the thump of a weighted Huggie hitting the bottom of the diaper bin, and the music from the mobile that hung above his crib indicating that everything was copacetic. In the course of her duties, Sally would muster the energy to engage in a one-way conversation with the baby, and the sounds I heard over the monitor were endearing if not precious.

"Wow, buddy, that was a stinky one! You're a stinky boy, huh? Yes, you are! Yes, you are!"

Our infant son would respond by cooing, wiggling like a fish, pumping his little legs like he was already riding a tricycle, and making it difficult for Sally to diaper and dress him in a fresh pair of pj's. Sometimes my curiosity would get the best of me, so I'd get up and see what all the commotion was about.

The presence of a newborn is special indeed. Caring for and holding a baby has a way of downplaying life's difficulties but even the cutest babies have a way of taxing their parents' endurance. The process of being awoken three or four times a night, clambering out of bed, sleepwalking into the nursery, and attending to a baby's needs requires stamina and patience in equal measure. As a light sleeper, I'm subject to being woken by the slightest sounds, and the baby's cries from the next room would wake me. They would startle me, in fact, no thanks to the baby monitor's position on the nightstand—on my side of the bed. Afterward, I would lie in bed, listening to the activity over the monitor, deciding whether to get up and lend a hand, or let nature take its course while I nodded off and fell back to sleep.

Having missed her audible cue to wake up, Sally hurried into the nursery with great trepidation. Meanwhile, I remained beneath the covers, listening for the telltale sounds that indicated my assistance wasn't required. As I lay there, my ears were straining to decipher the sounds I wasn't hearing; everything had grown very quiet—too quiet, in fact—when suddenly the silence was pierced by the sound of Sally's panic-stricken cry.

Launching from the bed, I bolted into the baby's room, dreading what I might discover. As I entered the nursery I wasn't met with a scene that I had come to expect. Ordinarily it felt as though I were entering a hygienic shrine. The images, even the fragrance of the nursery, projected a feeling of safety and comfort that only a parent can appreciate. Stacks of disposable diapers on the changing table, extra blankets, folded pajamas, and a variety of creams and ointments provided evidence that our child was well cared for. The scent of baby powder was always soothing, albeit frequently upstaged by the occasional dirty diaper (or two) that had been deposited in the hamper. Above the crib was a musical mobile consisting of farm animals and cutesy characters that only an infant would find fascinating. In the corner of the room was the rocking chair for nursing and the soft melodies that were sung in the hope that the baby would fall asleep. The walls were adorned with portraits of cherubs.

As I rushed into the room, I was overcome by a strange sensation. The air felt unusually cold and still. I felt flush with anxiety, seeing that Sally wasn't holding the baby; she was standing next to the crib holding her head in her hands, sobbing. Stepping slowly toward the crib, I looked down at our son, who was lying on his back, swaddled in his baby blue blanket. His eyes were slightly open, as was his mouth, and from a short distance he appeared to be asleep. Upon closer examination, however, I discovered that this was not our son—it was his corpse. Our child had passed away. Death had come, and in its wake there was little sign that life had ever existed. The vision before us was not only heart wrenching, it was haunting.

Picking him up carefully, I held our son close and felt that his body was limp and cold. Covering his nose and mouth with my lips, I breathed into him, hoping for a miracle. I saw his chest rise but the air escaped from his little mouth in a long, slow whisper. With that, I knew that any further attempt to revive him would be futile.

"He's gone," I uttered softly in despair. "He must have died in his sleep."

Having completed my crude forensic examination, all I could do was stand there in shock. My head acquired an instantaneous, throbbing migraine. My eyes became like faucets and my nose began to run profusely. As I hugged Sally in sorrow she collapsed in my arms, sobbing uncontrollably. It was the most devastating moment in our lives. Without warning or provocation, our infant son had died—while we were sleeping. *We slept through our son's passing?* Our immediate sensation was one of guilt: *Had we failed to respond to anything that might have saved him? Did he die quietly, or did he struggle?* The questions racing through our minds were merciless. The image of the baby lying there, the chill within the nursery—all of those horrible images remained with us for many, many months.

With two surviving children and a husband, Sally resumed her duties with great courage, but she suffered terribly while trying to overcome the loss of our child. For a mother, nothing could compare to what she had endured. Our girls were young, unable to fully grasp what had happened to their baby brother—or their parents, for that matter. Their mommy continued to take good care of them every day, while their daddy went off to work, just like before. While attending to her duties, Sally tried to wear a smile so as not to reveal the agony in her heart. Privately, she wept, behind closed doors, and did so for many months after the tragedy.

Several weeks after the baby's passing, Sally's friend called. When the phone rang, Sally was in the middle of one of her more melancholy moments. As she answered the phone, her friend detected Sally's distress and asked, "Are you okay?"

"I'm just having a bad day," she replied. "I've been thinking about the baby."

"You're not over that yet?" the friend asked.

The insensitive and thoughtless remark cut Sally to the core. Sadly, the harshness of her friend's comment paled in comparison to the truth in what had not been said, and the reality that Sally had been struggling to accept: *Life would go on.*

I suffered as well, but within days of the funeral I was back to work. The aftermath of so much activity and emotion left me feeling lost. I'd like to think that I concealed whatever challenges I was facing, but in all honesty, I felt like I was in a tunnel, bumping around in the darkness. Leaving the house before dawn provided me the concealment I needed to vent my emotions in solitude. The commuters beside me were too preoccupied with their morning coffee and talk radio to notice the guy in the next car—bawling, screaming, and trying with all his might to pull the steering wheel from the dashboard. I didn't want to lose control of my emotions at home; I needed be strong. For the first few weeks after the tragedy, I allowed myself several minutes each day for unrestricted grief. I cried and I cursed, I let it all hang out. I visited the cemetery during my lunch break. I couldn't bear the fact that our son was lying there alone without anyone to look after him. I brought flowers, tended to the grave, and prayed for the good Lord to look after him in heaven. Being at the grave site gave me comfort. I was still able to be a father to my son.

Looking back on that fateful night is like remembering a chapter from a novel that I read a very long time ago. The heartache has subsided, but what remains is an almost imperceptible void that lingers deep within me. It's been said that time heals all wounds, but the question of *why* such a tragedy occurred remained with me for years. Words cannot accurately describe the grief that Sally and I experienced after losing our son. It was a profound event, and yet, as strange as this may sound, I felt fortunate that he had passed before we were able to invest in him more of our heartfelt equity. I empathized for parents who lost their children to prolonged illness. I couldn't imagine the pain suffered by those who had to let go of a child that had grown to the age of five, eight, or eighteen years of age. In a strange sort of way, I felt fortunate for having to endure only a portion of the pain that many parents have had to overcome.

Coming to this realization helped me to put things in perspective and move on. Sadly, and as I endeavored to put my life back together, Sally continued to struggle with emotional challenges that were understandable yet difficult for me manage without losing the peace of mind that I had regained. For many months I tried desperately to pull her out of her doldrums but the task became greater than my capacity for endurance. The result of how the two us transitioned through this life-changing event created higher levels of stress. The partnership was collapsing. In lieu of resolving our differences by returning to that common ground, we stopped short and retreated to separate corners. I grew weary of the struggle as Sally and I grew further and further apart. In spite of the loss I felt compelled to move forward, and in the process my attitudes about life and death were changing. I became aware that I wasn't as concerned with living a *long life* as much as I was with living a *full one*. If and when it became my time to leave this world, then I too would move into the hereafter—just as my son had. In the meantime, I decided that I'd had enough. I'd taken my fifty lashes and it was time for me to move on. Having been through hell, I felt confident that I'd experienced the worst that life could offer. Whatever else destiny had in store was fine by me—*bring it on.*

As my emotions evolved I decided to embrace every opportunity as a vehicle upon which I was supposed to arrive at my next destination. In retrospect I now believe that the loss of my son marked not only an ending, but a beginning; it was the catalyst for things to come. As a result, I decided to live life in a manner that would permit me to meet my greatest expectations—while pursuing my dreams. In the years that followed I was able to accomplish more than I could have ever imagined, but like all things, it came at a price.

Over 100,000 civilian contractors served in Afghanistan during the War on Terror, and every one of them has a story that describes how and why they chose to embark upon such a perilous profession. For years, I was of the belief that I was different. I thought it was circumstance that had brought me downrange, and as a result, I thought I wasn't subject to the influences that affected the noncombatants who served side by side with those who fought to make the world a safer place. What I've learned since then, while writing this book, in fact, is that I was wrong. Like my colleagues who served in harm's way, separated from their families for months at a time while enduring difficult challenges—wondering on occasion if they'd make it home to see their loved ones again—I, too, have a story.

CHAPTER TWO

The Mourning After

The walls of my room were peppered with shrapnel. The TV had taken some hits, as had the reading lamp on the nightstand. The pillows on top of my bed were covered by dirt and debris. The explosion from the enemy rocket had nearly destroyed my sleeping container, and as I surveyed the damage I became conscious of the fact that my hand was pressing against the metal object beneath my shirt.

I remembered my mother's words. "Take this," she'd said. "I had it blessed by Father Mike. The chain and the crucifix are solid silver so don't lose it. I want you to wear this all the time, it'll keep you safe."

My mother is a woman of faith who believes in the power of prayer. The crucifix and chain weren't a gift; they were protection.

"Thanks, Mom," I said, kissing her cheek. "I'll wear it all the time."

I felt torn by my mother's gesture. I was thankful for her thoughts and prayers but I didn't want to reveal anything that might cause her to worry about me. The less she knew, the better.

Rosemary Catherine Lopreore was raised in New Orleans, Louisiana. She and her six brothers and sisters were reared by immigrant Italian parents who refused to speak anything but English to their children. My grandparents treasured their US citizenship and raised their offspring to respect and appreciate the ideals that prompted them to leave their birthplace for "The Land of Milk and Honey." The challenge they embarked on, however, came at a price, for in the pro-

9

cess of their cultural transition a part of my mother's Italian heritage was lost. I never knew my grandparents. They died while I was very young. But what I do know is that, like most of America's early immigrants, they were eager to become part of something they believed was greater than themselves. By the turn of the twentieth century, a multicultural conglomeration of immigrants had spawned a global phenomenon called "America" where people from around the world came in search of freedom and fortune.

I enjoyed hearing stories about my grandparents from my mother. She spoke often of how her father would lose his temper and use colorful phrases from the old country. Consequently, the only words in Italian that my mother ever learned were expletives and run-on sentences about pigs, prostitutes, and gypsies. Fortunately, she wasn't influenced by such outbursts, for like most Italians my mother was raised Roman Catholic and attended church each Sunday and every holy day of obligation. When she married my father, Edward Warren Cullen Jr., she remained faithful to her religious upbringing by maintaining her commitment to the church. With my three sisters and me in tow, my mother was determined to see to it that we embraced a level of respect and humility to a higher power that she believed would protect us and provide the foundation upon which we would lead compassionate and productive lives.

I'm biased, of course, but I've always felt that my mother is an exceptional woman. Despite being grounded by principles that are no longer fashionable, she doesn't judge others. One of her most admirable features is that she likes to laugh. She doesn't take herself (or life) too seriously, choosing instead to let things slide.

My mother is brave. She's a cancer survivor, and I'm confident that her faith and optimism aided in her recovery. I'm thankful for the positive impression that my mother made on me while I was growing up. Her uplifting spirit and unselfish nature played a great role in shaping my personality and compassion for others.

My father's name is Edward Cullen, and I need to pause for a moment to explain that there's no relation to the fictitious Edward Cullen, the vampire of Hollywood's *Twilight* film saga, starring Robert Pattinson. There was a time, however, when the cult film was enjoying its huge success, and our home phone rung off the hook with calls from curious teenagers.

"Are you *really* Edward Cullen?" the excited female adolescent asked.

"Yes, I'm Edward Cullen, may I help you?" my father replied.

"Oh my God!" screeched the young woman's voice over the telephone. "I can't believe I'm talking to *Edward Cullen*. It's really him!"

Edward Cullen, my father (not the vampire), is an academic. Throughout most of my youth, he made his living as an electrical engineer in the aerospace industry. In terms of personalities, my parents are nothing alike, but they have been married for over sixty years. My father has always been a good problem-solver who excels at thinking his way out of dilemmas that would discourage most people. He's retired, now, and spends much of his time reading, thinking, and napping. When he was younger, and despite the fact that he made his living figuring out complex engineering problems, he wasn't afraid to roll up his sleeves and get his hands dirty. I think he preferred the hands-on approach because it connected him with the people with whom he's always felt most comfortable: blue-collar, hardworking, salt of the earth. Watching my father connect and communicate with so many different types of people provided me with the tools I would need to succeed when I grew up. I was never interested in trying to match his academic prowess, but I acquired his talent for thinking on my feet and having the ability to react and adapt to change quickly.

I can say with confidence that thanks to my parents I've done all right; I've led a productive life—and I'm happy, most of the time. In terms of surviving some of my greatest challenges, the kind that I faced in Afghanistan, for example, my parents' influence played a role in that, too.

The morning after the rocket attack left an indelible memory. The events of that day were so profound, I can recall every detail of what I saw and felt. The bathroom in my sleeping container looked like someone had taken a sledgehammer to it. The porcelain toilet was broken in half, and the pedestal sink had been ripped from the wall and lay in pieces on the floor. The shower enclosure was completely destroyed, and there was a hole in the floor where the rocket had ended its flight. I can still hear the crackling of broken glass and ceramic tile beneath my boots.

The wall between the bathroom and the bedroom had deflected much of the blast, but a sizable cleanup effort would still be in order. The photos of my wife and children, tacked up on the wall, were punctured by a spray of shards from the explosion. Everything from the bedspread to the furniture, and even the curtain in front of the window, was covered by a fine layer of dust. A strange, stale odor was hanging in the air, so I reached over to pull open the window. As I tugged on the sash, the glass pane popped, and a spiderweb of fissures erupted from one side of the window to the other.

"Add that to the list," I said, with a sigh of frustration.

As I peered through the freshly cracked window I noticed a colleague named Cem (pronounced Gem) standing outside among a group of coworkers. His full head of jet-black hair hadn't been combed since he was thrown out of bed by the explosion. He looked tired, and his body language suggested he was still in shock. The expressions on everyone's faces that morning were the same: downcast, depressed, overwhelmed by the unexpected. No one could believe what had happened. Off to the side, several workers swapped stories about their experience during the mayhem. This was to be expected, but the level of nervous chatter, the hand-wringing, the *Oh-my-Gods*—all of these stress indicators suggested to me that people had forgotten we were in the middle of a war zone.

"I saw a huge, white flash outside of my window," a worker said with guarded excitement. "Then my window exploded into a million pieces. I'm lucky I wasn't cut by all the flying glass!"

"Something has to be done to protect us," remarked an agitated coworker. "We're sitting ducks out here!"

"No one cares about us," replied another. "We're expendable."

You got that right, I thought to myself. *And there's a line of fools just waiting to take our places.* I felt myself feeling bitter toward those who were traumatized by the events of that morning. Years later, I can see that my feelings of resentment were a defense mechanism that prevented me from succumbing to emotions I was fighting to suppress. Like my colleagues, I was shaken—but I couldn't show it; I held a position of leadership and was supposed to exude confidence. Unfortunately, it was neither my first rocket attack nor encounter with a battlefield tragedy. I had been through similar experiences while serving in the military. I had witnessed people agonizing over conditions they were powerless to change, and concluded that recounting the tragedy didn't help matters, it only made them worse. My remedy that morning was, therefore, to withdraw and allow others to process their grief in whatever way they felt was appropriate.

I should have been more sympathetic, but I wasn't; I was irritated by the incessant commiserating. I couldn't understand how so many people—educated engineers, no less—had underestimated our vulnerability. It angered me to hear the resentment they expressed, the futile search for a reason to blame something or someone besides the culprits themselves. Each of them had accepted the risk of coming to Afghanistan—which they all knew was a war zone—and they accepted that risk for the opportunity to earn a high salary.

Our camp was sitting on the outer edge of the FOB (forward operating base) and the prospect of being hit by a rocket was not only plausible, it was probable. In my view, it was only a matter of time before the law of averages caught up with us; this wasn't the first time our camp had been hit by an enemy rocket. In the past eighteen months, several rounds had impacted within the perimeter of our LSA (life support area), but fortunately, none of the explosions had resulted in loss of life. Some maintenance sheds were damaged and a truck or two were hit by shrapnel, but beyond that, there were never any serious consequences—not until that morning.

Working in Afghanistan was dangerous. Most of the contractors I associated with seemed to acknowledge that fact, but a surprising number weren't connecting the dots. They appeared blindsided whenever they came in close contact with anything life-threatening.

I was always cognizant of the fact that I might be injured or killed while working downrange. I never forgot where I was. It wasn't something I dwelled on, but in terms of stress management I had an advantage: I had served in combat and survived a tragedy of monumental proportion—the loss of an infant child. In the aftermath of the baby's death, I acquired (what I think was) a rather unique perspective: I surrendered my life to the will of destiny. I viewed my journey through life as if I were being transported downstream, floating on a river. The river could flow pleasantly or be swollen by a sudden storm, sweeping aside everything in its path. I viewed life as a force of nature I couldn't always control. Sometimes I would simply float on that river in a peaceful state, enjoying a pleasant ride, while other times I had to struggle just to keep my head above water.

Thinking about getting injured or being killed while employed in a war zone therefore seemed pointless. When it was my time to go, I would go, and there wasn't anything I, or anyone else, could do about it.

Surrendering to the notion that fate was in charge of my destiny didn't mean I wanted to die, or that I was at peace to the extent that my spiritual bags were packed in preparation for that journey into the afterlife. I simply chose not to burden myself with things I couldn't control.

This philosophy influenced my behavior on and off the battlefield. Knowing I couldn't control the worst possible scenario emboldened me to pursue the opposite end of the spectrum. In other words, when I wasn't working, I was enjoying life to the fullest. The Foreign Service Act of 1980 made available certain pay increases to contractor salaries, thereby providing access to income levels that were above and beyond what most blue and white-collar workers could hope to earn. The uplift salary incentives were adjusted per the job location and skill set of the worker. Driving a truck full of ammunition across Taliban-controlled territory (for example) paid more in six months than what most executives in the US could earn in a year. With uplift bonuses ranging from 40 to 200 percent above a person's prescribed salary, it's not hard to understand how people were influenced to assume and maintain employment in one of the most dangerous places on Earth.

The passage of time (along with writing this book) has enabled me to look back on the mind-set that dominated my thought process during my tenure as a war zone contractor. The decision to not burden myself with things I couldn't control went a bit deeper than the appearance of surrendering with ambivalence. In truth, I never felt certain whether I'd make it out of Afghanistan. I always hoped to, but the nature of my job meant assuming a great deal of risk. As such, I didn't map out a precise plan for my future; I didn't know how much of a future my job choice would allow me to have.

Seeing a section of our camp blown to pieces (including my room) was a wake-up call—and yet, I was fine. I had avoided injury, as a result of a schedule change. My colleague Mehmet and I were scheduled to arrive on the day before the attack, but extended meetings with clients had delayed our departure. We could have left our headquarters facility and arrived before dark, but we decided instead to postpone our trip until the following morning. The decision to wait until the next day may have spared Mehmet and me from being seriously injured, perhaps even killed. Mehmet's quarters were far worse

Photo from author's collection.

than mine; his container took the initial hit from the incoming rocket, whereas my container received damage from the secondary explosion.

While inspecting my room, I thought about my mother and how her prayers may have been responsible for my protection. I thought about my wife and how she would have to move on without me. How would she respond if I were permanently disabled? I dreaded the notion of being wheelchair-bound, paralyzed, or incapacitated. I felt certain that my wife would care for me, but I couldn't imagine the thought of being a burden to anyone. I thought about how fate may have played a role in safeguarding me from the attack. I began to wonder why things had turned out the way they had. *Why was I spared? Was it my destiny to experience so many challenges so I could gain some unique perspective, move on in life, and accomplish something else? What is my purpose?*

Conflicting thoughts were racing through my head. None them seemed to serve any positive end, and I felt myself sliding, overwhelmed by all the what-ifs.

"Get over it," I said quietly to myself. I took a breath, closed my eyes, and transitioned into that empty void where nothing matters. It was the place I went to avoid thinking about the things in my life that were unpleasant. I arrived in that dark state of denial. Suddenly, I felt neither relief for my good fortune nor concern over how close I may come to being injured or killed. Looking back, I can see how proficient I had become at avoiding thoughts that could turn into episodes of stress and depression. I had to maintain my edge, in order to cope with all the challenges that every warfighter and contractor has to deal with: family separation, loneliness, fatigue, fear, anger, guilt. All of these emotions had to be placed where they wouldn't jeopardize a person's safety and sanity: in the back of my mind.

I had another reason for not wanting to focus on myself that morning. His name was Murtaza. Murtaza was a colleague whose sleeping container was just forty feet from the enemy rocket's point of impact. Immediately after the explosion, a room-to-room search was conducted to check on the condition of all the workers. Murtaza was found lying on the floor next to his bed, writhing in pain from a small entry wound on his side. His colleagues rushed him to the base hospital, but the injury he sustained turned out to be grave, and Murtaza perished on the operating table. In the aftermath of the tragedy, all we could do was try to save ourselves from the grief, fear, and uncertainty of what lay ahead.

Murtaza's unfortunate passing hit everyone hard. Traumatized workers refused to reengage, while others became confrontational, blaming the company for neglecting to install proper safety measures that would defend them against attacks. They held nightly vigils and forwarded complaints about personnel safety to our corporate head-quarters. During the height of all the post-traumatic stress, I found myself feeling exasperated. I felt pity for those who were having dif-ficulty with their fear and the loss of a colleague, but their inability to put what happened in perspective was poisoning the workforce and negatively influenced our contractual obligations.

"What goes up, must come down," I lamented to Mehmet. "Once a rocket has been launched it's going to fall from the sky, that much is certain. I understand why people are scared," I continued, "but we can't offer guarantees for anyone's safety, not out here. We need to send home whoever isn't coping. They're demoralizing the workforce and threatening the company's interests."

To their credit, the company took a more diplomatic approach. A group of executives from the home office arrived on-site within days of the incident to assure the workers that additional safety measures would be employed—and they were. Concrete T-walls were built, and sandbags were installed throughout the LSA. In the days that fol-lowed, I came to realize that trying to make sense out of other peo-ple's reactions to the tragedy was futile. Murtaza had left a lot behind: his family, friends, and perhaps a long and prosperous life. He was nevertheless spared the burden his survivors were left to deal with. The survivors had the toughest job of all: they had to figure out how to move forward under the worst of circumstances.

The experience of working in Afghanistan was both tainted by tragedy and blessed by opportunity. After the war, I found that moving forward with my life required patience and a great deal of mental stamina. Years later, I still have moments when I wish I were back in Afghanistan. Life was simpler: we worked, we went on vacation, we lived, and we died. Most of what was happening around us was beyond our control. Part of me preferred it that way. Living within the oftentimes chaotic environment of a war zone seemed like a reasonable excuse for remaining somewhat disconnected from certain aspects of my life that were difficult to manage while I was downrange. More on that war story, later.

CHAPTER THREE

Living the Dream

On the morning of February 9, 1971, a magnitude 6.6 earthquake rocked the northeast section of the San Fernando Valley, just north of Los Angeles. California is known to have its share of seismic events, but this one was significant: sixty-five people were killed, over 2,000 were injured, and hundreds of millions of dollars in property damage was incurred.

Our house sustained substantial damage. The interior walls buckled and cracked, the exterior stucco ruptured from the structure's wooden framing, and the garden walls around our property toppled. It took several months to repair everything, and shortly before completion a strong aftershock undermined much of the work. It was a difficult period for the residents of the San Fernando Valley. Over time everything went back to normal. For some people the tragedy created opportunities upon which their lives would improve.

My father tackled most of the earthquake damage on our house; he was good at working with his hands, and his engineering background enabled him to figure out how everything went back together. Seeing that so many other people needed similar repairs, he went out on the weekends to earn some extra money. It was during this period that he had an epiphany that changed his life: realizing how much he had come to enjoy the independence of working on his own, my father resigned from the aerospace industry to become a self-employed building contractor.

In the early years of his new career, my father struggled. I recall several times when my mother didn't have money to buy groceries. She never lost faith in her husband, however, and my father never lost hope. I don't recall him ever looking worried or discouraged over the challenges he faced, he simply focused on the task before him and kept moving forward.

Over the years, my father's fertile mind never seemed to overlook an opportunity that could be exploited for profit. As a building contractor, he observed that nearly every construction project received support from one of several service companies that rented portable toilets, jobsite fencing, temporary field offices, and temporary power equipment. As an electrical engineer, his attention was naturally drawn to the temporary power equipment that provided electricity to the jobsites. The more he studied the business, the more intrigued he became. Equipped with as much knowledge about power distribution as Colonel Sanders knew about frying chicken, my father wagered that he could start a similar type of business—and do well. As it turned out, he did very well. But I can't give my father all the credit; he had help from a movie star who became the president of the United States. The celebrity was none other than Ronald Reagan.

Reagan served as the California state governor from 1967 to 1975 before his two terms in office as the US President from 1981 through 1989. After narrowly defeating Gerald Ford for his first term in office, Reagan was reelected for a second term by winning every single electoral vote in all fifty states—except one, in the home state of his opponent, former Vice President Walter Mondale of Minnesota. President Reagan's reelection to a second term was a landslide of epic proportion, and with it followed a robust US economy that hasn't been matched since his presidency. The Reagan years provided a steady growth period from which many small businesses sprouted and prospered. Like the California Gold Rush, whereby opportunistic businessmen made their fortunes selling pickaxes and shovels to prospectors, the building boom in California offered anyone with a pickup truck and a hammer the means to earn a good living.

Within ten years of leaving the aerospace industry, my father's entrepreneurial idea had morphed into a corporation that employed over thirty personnel. Our company had a fleet of trucks, three branch offices in Southern California, and a fourth office in Las Vegas. Throughout the process, my dad and I worked side by side, and the rewards were great—both financially and personally.

"It's you and me against the world, son!" my father would say, as we drove to the next jobsite. The wind in his hair and the dirt on his trousers were a testament to having achieved the personal success he had striven to obtain.

Periodically, our company would receive an order to set up equipment on US military installations. I was fond of working on the military bases because of my admiration for our men and women in uniform. I had thought about enlisting in the Navy after high school but pursued my college education instead. It was one of my few regrets at the time, but I quietly rationalized that my life in the private sector was fulfilling. I had nearly everything I wanted, and could pursue the rest at my leisure.

One day, our company had a job at the Naval Construction Battalion Center at Port Hueneme, just north of Los Angeles. Once inside the base, I noticed sailors running and singing cadence and larger groups of sailors mustered in formation. Behind all the hustle and bustle of the sailors were warships docked alongside the pier, brimming with activity. It was breathtaking. As a boy, I had developed an attraction to all things associated with the US Navy. The battleships and the sailors who manned them seemed larger than life. My father, who served in the Navy during the Korean War, stowed some of his old keepsakes in the closet. Among the items was a woolen peacoat with last name and service number stenciled on the inside of the jacket. I also found his white sailor's cap, an old canvas belt, and some photos of him wearing his dress blue crackerjack uniform. The look of pride on my father's face was something I hadn't seen before. He appeared young and vibrant. Seeing that look of confidence assured me that whatever my dad was doing in the Navy, it must have been great. From that moment forward, I was convinced I, too, would join the Navy one day, and partake in the adventures that my father's photo indicated.

Among my father's keepsakes was a leather-bound book entitled *The Bluejacket's Manual,* which described in detail all the things a sailor would need to know during his/her naval career. After mastering such literary classics as *One Fish, Two Fish, Red Fish, Blue Fish* and *Horton Hears a Who,* I began reading *The Bluejacket's Manual.* I couldn't comprehend many of the words or the terminology, but the pictures and the content left an impression on me that would last a lifetime. I dreamed of wearing the uniform of a sailor, sailing the deep blue sea, and flying a jet off the deck of an aircraft carrier.

Years later, while driving our company truck next to a US warship, I was entranced by the enormity of what I was experiencing. Colorful signal flags hung from the halyards, and I could hear announcements broadcast over the ship's PA system. On the stern flew our national ensign, the American flag, snapping in the cool, salt-scented breeze. Everything taking place appeared well organized and carried out with a sense of purpose. The images that were instilled in me as a boy came flooding back. It was an intoxicating moment. Whatever I had achieved up to that point in my life seemed to pale in comparison.

I should have been satisfied with everything I had going for me, but I wasn't. I was never satisfied as a young adult, and I've paid dearly for it. I think I inherited that trait from my father, the inquisitive engineer who is always trying to improve things. By thirty-four years of age, I had been married for ten years, Sally and I had two little girls, ages seven and five, and we were living in a custom home I had built with my own hands. Our quality of life was good, everyone was happy, and the future looked bright. Whatever I had achieved, personally and professionally, should have been enough to satisfy most people—but not me. I wanted more.

Against Sally's wishes, and to my father's astonishment, I enlisted in the United States Navy Reserve. Having earned success in the private sector, I wanted to test myself by doing things more meaningful than earning money and living in a nice house.

Sally wasn't keen on the idea. She felt that venturing out in pursuit of a boyhood dream (which could potentially impact our family business or get me killed) was irresponsible and foolish. Stubbornly, I refused to acknowledge how serving my country might be counterproductive to my best interests. Moreover, I felt confident that enlisting in the Navy Reserve wouldn't turn my life around, at least not completely.

Boy, was I wrong. About a decade later I would find myself forward-deployed to Iraq and Afghanistan wearing body armor and humping weapons and ammo.

The Navy recruiter placed me where he thought I could add instant value, by assigning me to serve with the naval construction force, home of the Navy Seabees. As a private building contractor, I was tailor-made for duty with the Seabees, who, as the Navy's forward-deployed combat construction force, gained notoriety building airfields and bases on remote islands in the Pacific during WWII. Their can-do spirit still resonates through the military, and I felt proud to be a part of such a historic group.

My transition into the Navy went well. I wore the uniform with pride and was well on my way to making progress with my new endeavor. After only a few months into my enlistmen, however, Sally and I lost our infant son to crib death.

I was devastated by the loss, but the Navy proved to be a therapeutic outlet for my grief. By exercising daily and immersing myself in preparing for the following month's activities, I was given a much-needed distraction. The healing process not only provided an outlet to rebuild my spirit, it enlightened me to the fact that I had discovered something I enjoyed doing and was good at.

My self-induced therapy and its positive results offered little in terms of relief for Sally, who spent most of her time being a mother and a housewife. As my life was moving forward, she was anchored to a routine that prohibited her from finding time to participate in other activities. Throughout each day, she would pass the empty room where our son had slept, and as one might imagine, blocking the connection between the room and her loss was not an easy feat. Meanwhile, the progress I seemed to be making wasn't helping her recovery, and as a result, she became resentful. It probably seemed as if I'd gotten over the baby's passing, but I was only doing what my instincts had compelled me to do: survive.

My recovery program provided me with an unfair advantage. My life was moving forward while Sally was being left behind. Life is never fair, and I'm a believer that relationships are never 50/50; they're 90/10, whereby one of the two parties carries the load while the other works on coming up to speed. Throughout the course of every relationship, the dynamics between couples have a tendency to shift. The balance of responsibility between partners is rarely equal, therefore, it moves back and forth. Whenever the scales tip in favor from one or the other for too long, however, trouble is soon to follow.

As the months went by, Sally continued to struggle with her heartfelt loss. She gave her best effort at putting the tragedy behind her, but it's not something your average person is equipped to handle. Statistically speaking, most couples who suffer the loss of a child to sudden infant death syndrome fail to keep their relationships intact. My preference would have been for us to beat those odds, but we didn't, and eventually we divorced.

During a dip in the economy, I left my father's electrical contracting business and went to work for my brother-in-law, Claudio. Claudio, a native Italian from Rome, met my sister Susan while she was touring Italy. Within two years of their meeting, they were married and set up house in LA. Shortly after learning to speak English, Claudio parlayed his handsome looks, Italian charm, and the business smarts of my sister into a marble and granite import/supply business that catered to high-end builders, commercial projects, and celebrities throughout the western United States. Within a few years, Claudio and Susan's business was booming.

The business required us to make periodic trips to Italy, to purchase slabs and tiles for inventory and special projects. My Italian roots must have been yearning for some nourishment, because that first trip to Italy changed my life. I fell in love with the Italian culture, the language, Italy's history and architecture, and, of course, the food. After returning from Italy, I enrolled in night school, to learn how to speak Italian. I was a mediocre student, but with the aid of some audio instruction I was able to master the basics while commuting to and from work. Years later, I left my brother-in-law's business and teamed up with a marble installation company. Within several months of starting my new job, I headed to Italy to find some material for the business. After flying into Rome, I took a northbound train to Tuscany and set up my base of operations in the seaside town of Forte Dei Marmi. I chose Forte Dei Marmi for two reasons, the first having to do with its proximity to the marble factories of Pietrasanta and Carrara, where most of my business was done. My second reason for choosing Forte Dei Marmi was because I found it charming. The town, which consists of an upscale retail district within a seaside community, reminded me of a combination of Beverly Hills and Malibu.

Forte Dei Marmi sits along the Mediterranean, below the majestic marble quarries of the Apuan Alps. Michelangelo selected pristine

Photo from author's collection.

blocks of white marble from these mountains, and from those quarries hauled twenty-ton blocks of stone by oxen cart to the oceanside pier at Forte Dei Marmi. The blocks were loaded onto ships that sailed south, along the Italian peninsula, before heading inland via the Tiber River into Rome. Today, Forte Dei Marmi is a resort community. The quaintness of its historic past is accentuated by sprawling beaches that serve as a segue to some of Italy's finest fashion outlets: Gucci, Prada, and Dolce & Gabbana are among some of the exquisite boutiques that line Forte Dei Marmi's marble-clad sidewalks. The combination of beaches, upscale hotels, outdoor dining establishments, and high-end retail outlets draws hundreds of thousands of tourists each year.

After spending the morning looking at inventory for the marble shop, I returned to my hotel to clean up and have some lunch. Deciding on a restaurant along the seashore, I entered an enoteca (locally produced wine bar) and was seated at a table. Unlike most American eating establishments, where the objective is to feed as many customers during the lunch or dinner shift as possible, the Italians have a more civil approach to dining: meals are meant to be enjoyed and clients are not encouraged to rush. While waiting to be served, I was soaking up the atmosphere. A rich aroma wafted from the kitchen throughout the restaurant. The sound of the *pizzaiolo's* spatula slicing under the freshly made pizza, and the pop of a cork being pulled from a wine bottle couldn't have been choreographed more precisely. While surveying my surroundings, I noticed a waitress standing off to the side. She stood out, first, because I hadn't seen many women working in restaurants up to that point, and secondly, she was very attractive. It was as if Gina Lollobrigida had transported through time to work in a Tuscan café.

As a boy, I dreamed of marrying an Italian beauty like my mother. Italian women are notorious for fussing over their men, and my dad and I were no exception. We were called to table at every meal. My mother and sisters served us, and we were never expected to clear a plate. My sisters did the dishes while my father and I retired to the den to watch the evening news. While unlikely that such a routine might exist (today) in modern American society, back in the day, there was nothing unusual or "sexist" about such behavior—at least not in our household. My share of chores included taking out the trash, scooping the dog poop, and helping my father with the yard work. I'll admit that there was a downside to being waited on by my mother and sisters for most of my life: to this day, I don't know how to cook anything that requires more than a toaster, microwave oven, or skillet—but I can eat. I'm a good eater.

Gina Lollobrigida, aka Barbara to her family and friends, appeared to be gliding on a cushion of air, unfazed by the hectic activity within the restaurant. She moved with the grace of a sophisticate, while her male colleagues darted in and out of the kitchen. Her Mona Lisa smile suggested that she was confident, content, and yet approachable. Her skin had been darkened by the sun, and her black hair shimmered in the sunlight that streamed through the outdoor pergola. Her tight-fitting black pants revealed the silhouette of her derriere, which was hard not to notice. I was smitten.

Barbara tells a story that is equally intriguing. Having noticed me when I entered the restaurant, she was impressed by the tall, confident-looking foreigner. Correctly assessing that I was an American (we Yanks tend to dress a certain way), she set her sights on making my acquaintance and informed one of her male colleagues that she would serve me.

"Ma che fai! Quello tavolo e mio!" the waiter proclaimed. *What are you doing, that's my table!*

"I've got this," she responded in her native tongue. "In fact," she added, straightening her apron and combing back her lustrous, dark hair with her fingers, "I'm going to marry that man."

The rest of the story is romantic yet interwoven with drama, pain, and the pursuit of forbidden pleasures that began with Adam and Eve in the Garden of Eden. My first encounter with Barbara was as enchanting as any chapter ever written for a dime-store romance novel. Three years later, we were married, and we've been together ever since.

For years, I believed that unlike a lot of contractors who worked downrange, I didn't have any special reason for being there. I wasn't unemployed, nor compelled to look for a job on the other side of the world. I didn't owe back taxes to the IRS, and I wasn't running away from a bad marriage; I had been remarried to Barbara for several years and we were very content. From my point of view, the climate of my life had changed for the better. I had survived several years of unfavorable conditions, and the sun was shining upon me again.

What I've figured out, since then, is that nothing happens by accident or coincidence. Wherever we happen to be in life is the result of a certain path that we choose to embark upon. The path I chose was the result of my desire to achieve a number of objectives. In exchange for accomplishing my goals, I had to make some choices. Some of the choices were conscious while others were made without the investment of much thought at all.

By remaining true to my desire to experience as much as I could in life, to test myself to the limits of my capability, I was rewarded with results that were reassuring and profitable. I was in my element, doing my best work, and being compensated well in every way imaginable: financially, mentally, and spiritually. In a manner of speaking, I was living the dream.

Like all dreams, however, eventually I woke up and realized that there were parts of my life that weren't as accurate as the perception being broadcast. Like a glorified Facebook account, where people's virtual, idyllic lives conveniently overlook the day-to-day burdens that all humans endure, there were parts of my life that I chose neither to publish nor even think about.

CHAPTER FOUR

Investments, Dividends, and Returns

The other contractors and I, who transitioned from our comfortable lives in America to the austere conditions in Afghanistan, faced many challenges. During the most challenging period of America's Great Recession (Dec 2007 through June 2009) millions of Americans were hanging by a thread: debt was piling up, taxes weren't being paid, relationships impacted by financial calamity were falling by the wayside and people were losing hope. As a result of the tens of thousands who sought refuge by taking jobs in a war zone, the mass exodus from the Land of Milk and Honey to the Land of Not Quite Right was something to behold.

Upon my release from active duty, I was faced with the prospect of either restarting my civilian career in LA or doing something else. Having found a job opportunity in Europe, I opted to leave the US and see what destiny had in store. Within the first three months, I was presented with an offer to oversee construction projects in Afghanistan. I accepted the position in hope of parlaying the opportunity into something better. In exchange for my investment I received far more than I could have imagined—and not all of it was good.

I returned to Afghanistan as a civilian contractor, aboard a commercial airliner, carrying a laptop computer and wearing a pair of 5.11 tactical gear cargo pants. It wasn't the same as flying aboard a C-130 with a hundred other guys, toting weapons and wearing full battle-rattle. Setting foot into the war zone unarmed was also far less glamorous. I didn't have the thousand-yard stare that combat-fatigued troops acquired. Instead, I was grimacing with pain from the friction burns on my rear end, the result of excessive fidgeting in my economy-class seat.

Kabul, Afghanistan, was not unfamiliar territory. I'd been there before while serving on active duty with the Navy. On this trip and for the rest of whatever time I'd be spending downrange, I'd be alone. I wouldn't have any battle buddies nor the assurance that armed and well-trained colleagues would be looking out for me. My situation wasn't unique, however. There were literally tens of thousands of civilian contractors who would do as I did: leave the safety of their homes for the uncertainty of what lay ahead.

The contractor's arrival in-country included a list of concerns that would give anyone pause: *Will my pick-up from the airport be waiting for me? What am I supposed to do if no one shows? Where did I put that guy's cell phone number? Will my cell phone even work?*

To my relief, a NATO coworker was waiting for me outside the customs area. Upon meeting him, I didn't overreact. I didn't smile or offer any hint that I was glad to see him. I simply said hello, shook his hand, and got about the business of doing whatever came next. The environment seemed familiar, but the circumstances were different. I tried not to appear paranoid, but I wasn't comfortable entering a potentially hostile environment without a weapon. I would later discover that the threat condition at Kabul Airport was minimal, but my experience up to that point had always included carrying an M4 rifle and a pistol with enough rounds to hold off a small attack.

From the terminal, we took a back door directly to the airfield tarmac, where I threw my gear into what would be the first of several hundred Toyota SUV Land Cruisers that would transport me all over

Afghanistan—for the next six years. Of all the companies that benefited from the war, Toyota Industries must have done exceptionally well; their vehicles were everywhere.

As we drove along the taxiway, we made our way from the Kabul-Afghanistan International Airport, aka KAIA (*kai-yah*), to the NATO airport of debarkation, or APOD. The NATO side of the airport on KAIA represented one of several International Security Assistance Force (ISAF; *eye-saff*) bases in Kabul—and if you're already bored by all the explanations in parentheses, then welcome to the world of abbreviations, acronyms, made-up words, and phraseology that exists within the military's unofficial dictionary. People who work in our world throw these abbreviated phrases around like nicknames. I found it ironic to note how rarely people understood what the letters within the acronyms or abbreviations represented. For example: An HMMWV (high mobility multipurpose wheeled vehicle) is a Humvee. Everyone knows what a Humvee is, but if presented with the letters HMMWV most people couldn't tell you what each letter represented.

The NATO base at KAIA was home to over 4,000 multinational coalition forces. ISAF was represented by over fifty nations who made up the coalition. Before the war, the facility served as commercial cargo terminal for the Kabul airport. During the Russian occupation, the airfield served as a forward operating base that came under constant attack from Afghan rebel forces. By the time the Russians quit the conflict, the airport was in a state of ruin, pockmarked by bullets and ravaged by looters.

Among these battle-fatigued buildings was a series of complexes that were renovated by the coalition forces. The old terminal became a restaurant, an administration building served as the headquarters complex, and several utility buildings were put to use as maintenance sheds. The rest of the camp consisted of containerized housing units and retail shops. A power farm with six diesel generators sat in the middle of the camp, and the hum of their engines could be heard twenty-four hours a day.

The color of KAIA was different from the typical US military base. Coalition troops from all over the world wore battle fatigues that defined their countries of origin. The US troops were easiest to identify—I'd worn those BDUs (battle dress uniforms) only months before. The US Marines were one of the first to introduce the digital design onto the battlefield, and within those camouflaged patterns were the globe and anchor, the symbol of the Marine Corps. The Australian forces had a peculiar camouflage pattern that resembled bunnies and jelly beans and the French special forces wore oversized berets that hung below the ear. Some of the NATO troops were more squared away (professional-looking) than others. The Belgian and the French forces reflected their military bearing, as did the US forces: clean-shaven, physically fit, ready to rock. Members of the Swedish Air Force were permitted to wear beards and their blond hair below the collar. I'm not suggesting that the Swedes were any less capable than our US Marines; they simply appeared more relaxed. They smiled a lot more, too. I suspect they were more content going native, ignoring the status quo, and marching to the beat of their own drum.

Our ten-minute commute from the airport terminal ended at my new home, a 160-unit complex of eight-by-twenty-foot containerized housing modules double-stacked side by side. A roof structure provided a weathertight seal and covered the long corridors. I estimate that there must have been ten such complexes throughout the camp. Each sleeping unit could accommodate up to four personnel.

My first roommate was a Canadian named Ted. Ted had long, shaggy blond hair and a tan. He may have looked like a California surfer, but as he hailed from Ottawa. I couldn't say whether he'd ever seen the Pacific Ocean. Despite being roommates, Ted and I were never close; he wasn't very chatty, so I kept to myself. Within two months of my arrival, Ted decided he'd had enough of Afghanistan and went home. He had been working in-country for about eighteen months and was ready to call it quits. Ted's departure was insightful in that he knew when it was his time to go. I rarely met anyone who could arrive at the same conclusion as pragmatically as he did. He may have looked like some laid-back surfer dude, but he was sharp, and had a good head on his shoulders. On the eve of his departure, Ted spoke of wanting to finish his bachelor's degree in civil engineering and marry the woman who'd been waiting for him. It sounded like a good plan.

Over the years, I got to know quite a few contractors, but unlike Ted, very few of them returned home of their own volition; the salaries we earned were simply too good to walk away from. Invariably, contracts would run out, suspicious wives would demand their mischievous husbands return home, and troublemakers would be terminated for cause. For the most part, however, people stayed; they didn't want to miss out on an opportunity to make hay while the sun shines.

During the peak years of the Afghanistan conflict, most of the world was drowning in a global recession. Meanwhile, civilian contractors downrange never felt so much as a ripple within the pool of prosperity they had discovered—unless they overindulged, which many did. For this reason, people accepted the risks of living in the combat zone over returning home to face fewer opportunities, less pay, and unemployment. Ironically, most contractors (including me) rarely gave so much as a second thought as to the actual consequences of what we felt was a wise investment in our futures; the magnitude and duration of our sacrifices, along with the volume and caliber of the returns, seemed aptly justified.

Like any high-risk, high-return investment scheme, however, those who spent years in Afghanistan never knew whether the investment they'd made would yield the results they were hoping for. Adding yet another element of risk to this complex portfolio was the fact that *the returns* weren't always measured in dollars. After the war, many contractors would discover they weren't the only people who had been impacted by years of separation. The people around them had changed as well.

Despite its simplicity, the austere living conditions on KAIA weren't uncomfortable. Everything I needed was provided: food, shelter, and security. For the first few months, I stayed in my room and watched DVDs while ironing my clothes. The laundry service didn't use conventional dryers, so everyone's clothes were returned looking like they'd been tied in knots. Despite being in the middle of a war zone I wasn't about to look like I had slept in my clothes; my mother had raised me better than that.

Spending those evenings alone prompted thoughts of the life I had left behind. Sally had remarried and my children were well cared for, so much so that they didn't seem to have any concerns for what their father might be doing in Afghanistan. I attempted to stay in touch, but there didn't seem to be much interest on the other end. They received my birthday and Christmas presents but rarely acknowledged them. Whenever I called, the kids were pleasant, cordial, and respectful, but no one seemed curious about my unusual situation. The excitement of talking to Dad seemed preoccupied by events I had become disassociated with, and within a relatively short period of time I was a stranger to my own children. I felt heartbroken yet deserving of the pain I had inflicted on myself. I wasn't displeased by their good fortune, nor their ability to adapt well in my absence. Perhaps it was fate dealing me my just rewards, but I cannot recall a time in my life when I felt so alone. Adjusting to the heartache required a margin of separation, and for a period of time I ceased all contact with my children entirely. Sadly, none of them seemed to notice, but in all fairness, I suspect that they too were trying to manage a difficult situation within their own set of limitations.

Over time, I was able to compartmentalize whatever caused me to feel sad or depressed. Lingering in self-pity or sorrow would threaten to distract my attention and make me complacent. On the battlefield, complacency can kill someone faster than a bullet, with accidents and mishaps caused by people simply not paying attention.

Staying busy every day wiped away the opportunity for unpleasant thoughts to distract and depress me. It also made me so tired that by the end of the day all I wanted to do was crawl into bed and fall asleep. I felt fortunate that I was so tired I didn't have the energy to take inventory of everything I'd lost in pursuit of the life I was living.

The math was easy but the sum didn't amount to anything worth putting down on paper: I was one side of the world, my kids were on the other, and life was going on.

Anyone who has served in combat will agree that one of the secrets to survival is maintaining a positive attitude. Appreciating whatever you have (versus complaining about whatever you don't) goes a long way. Living on the NATO camp at KAIA could have been worse; we could have been getting bombed every night, like some of my contractor buddies were when they served in Iraq. We had it made, on KAIA; we had bars serving alcohol after 7:30 p.m., and if you got tired of the regular food served at the DFAC (*dee-fak: dining facility*) there were several establishments where you could order something different: Thai food, pizza, chicken wings, or a burger and fries.

Within every military conflict there are a series of political objectives, and in Afghanistan, politics played heavily on how the war was fought. One of the perks offered by the US and its coalition forces included allowing local merchants to set up various retail outlets within the military bases. KAIA had a local bazaar that featured souvenirs, electronics, DVDs, and handmade carpets. The layout of shops consisted of containerized retail stores known to the contractors and warfighters as the "Hajji shops."

A Hajji is someone who has made a religious pilgrimage to Mecca, the birthplace of the prophet Muhammad, whose teachings are the foundation of Islam. Embarking upon and completing the pilgrimage to Mecca is the most important commitment a Muslim can make to his/her faith, so, in a manner of speaking, referring to someone as a Hajji—with or without understanding the importance of the title—and/or dismissing its relevance—is disrespectful. Warfighters and contractors were known to routinely deviate from the rules of social protocol and political correctness. In the absence of respect or concern for people they either disliked or didn't understand, they often used condescending names and titles like this one.

All of that being said, the Hajji shops offered an opportunity for people to take their minds off the war . Most of the trinkets offered by the merchants weren't worth taking home, but for the serious shoppers there was always a healthy selection of newly released Hollywood feature films. Of course, they were pirated DVDs, which meant the quality was iffy, at best. I routinely witnessed contractors and military folks harassing the local merchants, complaining they'd received a DVD that either didn't work or was of such poor quality that it couldn't be watched without frequent distraction. I wondered if these Fortune 500 investors expected to receive high-definition picture quality and THX Digital Sound for their two-dollar purchase. In exchange for their inconvenience, whining customers were encouraged to take another DVD at no charge. Being shrewd businesspeople, the unhappy clients would think they were getting the better end of the deal—despite how poor their new selection was guaranteed to be. Meanwhile, the clever local merchants were always glad to make an exchange. Their penny-pinching clients would inevitably select two or three more DVDs before leaving their establishment.

This type of high-level Wall Street trading went on all the time. The store owners, who were buying stolen merchandise for ten cents on the dollar, and making a sizable profit, could afford to make concessions with disgruntled customers who always came back for more.

Despite the creature comforts at KAIA, life within the old airport was surrounded by hazards. Afghanistan is known for having one of largest concentrations of land mines per square meter on the planet. During the Soviet occupation of Kabul, KAIA was under constant attack by the mujahideen. To keep their attackers at bay, the Soviets mined both the perimeter and the interior of the airfield. When they quit the conflict, the Russians left all their handiwork in place. Thirty years later, KAIA still bore testament to the battles that took place around and within the old Russian stronghold. Beyond the rusted hulks of armored personnel carriers and broken-down airplanes were thousands of land mines. Safeguarding the reclaimed property involved a special breed of civilian contractors who de-mined every square meter of the airport that would eventually be repurposed for the reconstruction of KAIA (North) in its entirety—which occurred, in fact, and was commissioned in 2009.

The de-mining operations were performed by civilian contractors dressed in a pair of yellow or blue coveralls, so they could be seen from a great distance. They also wore body armor and helmets to protect themselves from any exploding debris, but the superficial outer garments did little to offset the effects of any sizable charges. Thus, casualties among the de-miners were common. During these operations, the de-mining contractors would accumulate a healthy collection of unexploded ordnance. Transporting these assets off-base was too risky, so they detonated them in place, every day at 3:00 p.m.

Photo from author's collection.

The frequency and duration of the controlled dets (detonations) was a reminder that the weapons of war could be powerful and persuasive. The Russians had left tons of ordnance behind at KAIA, and the variety of explosives they abandoned ranged from small munitions and rockets to 500-pound cluster bombs. Before the insurgents caught on to the fact that we conducted controlled dets at 3:00 p.m. daily (after several weeks of continuous controlled dets, KAIA was actually attacked by enemy mortars at 3:00 p.m. on the dot, *go figure*), no one ever knew how big the daily explosions would be. Sometimes they sounded like nothing more than a distant blast being detonated in a canyon, while other times the sky would erupt in a double-tap of thunder as the immense explosion was followed by a shock wave that broke the sound barrier. In summary, both controlled detonations and spontaneous explosions (caused by actual attacks) were unnerving, to say the least. Most people never actually got used to explosions, especially when they impacted at close range.

Civilian contractors brought great credit upon themselves by consistently and successfully executing their work under adverse conditions. One of the things that impressed me most was the speed with which we accomplished everything. War zones don't offer the time that's always needed to make a good decision or complete projects as planned. Time is a luxury on the battlefield, and getting things done quickly became the standard operating procedure. As a manager of airfield construction projects, my job was to maintain progress without being impacted by the confines of a fully operational air campaign. Repairing a runway or providing a parking apron that could accommodate more aircraft (while airplanes were taxiing and taking off all around us) meant the difference between running a defense campaign and getting the upper hand against our adversaries. Our construction teams took great pride in the work we did, and nothing motivated us more than to see a thumbs-up from the pilots as they taxied away on a new section of pavement that we provided.

In no time at all, I came to realize I was good at what I did. I felt comfortable working within the trade I grew up with, and at ease working with the military. It felt as though I had come full circle. I started out as a civilian contractor in the private sector, did a couple of tours of duty in uniform, and returned downrange as a civilian contractor. The experience had enabled me to combine the two worlds I had left behind (private contracting and the US military) to create yet another world where I would succeed: civilian contracting.

Most people changed while they were downrange. I know I did. You changed to protect yourself and to cope with the challenges of an unusual and stressful environment. Not everyone changed, however. There were a few people who were exceptions to the rule, and some of them were extraordinary human beings. After Ted left KAIA I acquired a new roommate named Lorenzo. Lorenzo was a lieutenant colonel in the Spanish Air Force who had been seconded to the NATO agency that employed me. Serving as the contracting officer on my project meant that Lorenzo would have to spend much of his time working with me. This worked out well, for Lorenzo and I had a lot in common. Like me, Lorenzo was easygoing and never took life too seriously. As an officer in the Spanish Air Force, he was dedicated to serving his country and performed his job with precision. Lorenzo was also a bit of a character. He was always joking around, drawing cartoons on the whiteboard in our office and making fun of me. Most of the time he had me in stitches, but sometimes he was like an old mother hen; he fussed at me whenever I ignored him, which was normal; roommates don't always agree on everything.

The eight-by-twenty-foot containerized sleeping unit that Lorenzo and I shared was cozy but small. Out of respect for each other's privacy, we installed a curtain between our sleeping areas. The fabric barrier enabled one person to sleep while the other read a book or watched TV. If neither of us was asleep, we'd leave the curtain open and have conversations, like two brothers sharing the same room. After being together for several months, we established the type of bond that occurs between colleagues who are separated from their families. As military veterans, we shared the same core values. We were also both Catholics who trusted their faith in God and endeavored to be compassionate with others. Truthfully however, my level of compassion and sensitivity paled in comparison to Lorenzo's. His ability to be unconditionally human in the face of such adverse conditions was humbling.

Sometimes Lorenzo would have to wait outside the front gate to receive shipping documents for the projects we were overseeing. While waiting, he would usually encounter a small group of local children who were always hanging around the main gate, selling chewing gum or trying to score something from whomever they could persuade to feel sorry for them—which was nearly everyone, since the Afghan kids were a pathetic-looking lot. Most people shunned the little mudbugs, who were dirty and had runny noses, indicating that they were sick. Despite whatever condition they happened to be in, Lorenzo never denied those children. He was like the Pied Piper, keeping all his little street rats in line. He would captivate their attention with stories and antics. The children were enamored by the attention, and in return, they showed him a level of respect that was not afforded others.

One evening, as we were about to turn in, Lorenzo told me he had learned the names of all the kids, and that he was planning to bring them inside the base for some pizza and sodas. For the next few weeks, and every night before we retired, Lorenzo recounted the same story as if he'd never spoken of it before.

"I've heard that story, Lorenzo...a hundred times," I groaned. "You told me that one last night, and the night before that. Don't you have any other bedtime stories?"

Lying in his bed, pondering the ceiling above, Lorenzo would ignore me. He just kept on talking about these little kids as if they were his own. One day, I went to grab a pizza for lunch, and there was Lorenzo, with eight little Afghan kids, munching away on pizza and drinking sodas. It was a trip. Lorenzo never forgot those kids. He would go home for his R&R and return with secondhand clothes that his children in Spain had outgrown. One day, we were sitting outside the front gate, and he pointed out a local boy who was running around in a pair of his son's old pajamas. When he returned to Afghanistan, after going home for Christmas, Lorenzo brought back several new pairs of sneakers for the kids. He went as far as buying shoes equipped with Velcro, in case the kids couldn't tie their own.

I never allowed myself to get that close to the children in Afghanistan. I found it too heartbreaking. I was a softie and they knew it. Whenever they'd ask for something, whether it was a bottle of water or a dollar, I'd give it to them, and within seconds of snatching it from my hand they'd demand more. I couldn't satisfy them; no one could. All of them were living below the poverty level. Most of them had never seen a bathtub, and they were ignorant of even the simplest traditions that most children instinctively understand, like saying please or thank you. It was pitiful to see children growing up without attention from their parents or elders. They were on their own most of the time. Some wouldn't even smile when a gesture of kindness was bestowed upon them; they were too busy trying to figure out how to acquire more.

It broke my heart to see such displays of irrepressible need. I never expected to be thanked, but my dismay was the result of the children's needs being insatiable; the slightest gesture of kindness would serve as a catalyst to demand something else. In the beginning, I would give whatever I had, and then struggle to free myself from their persistent demands. Sometimes the little hoodlums would curse at me, using colloquial expletives they learned from US troops. At first, I was taken aback by the accuracy with which they could let such vulgarities fly. After several unpleasant episodes, I decided to limit my contact. By ignoring the street kids, I avoided the occasion to be drawn into the drama they were so skilled at manipulating. However effective my tactics were, it troubled me knowing I could sink to such levels of ambivalence and still sleep at night. It's not easy denying a child in need, but sadly, I became good at that, too.

Lorenzo's patience and compassion for those children was extraordinary; his generosity seemed to have no limits. As for the children, they didn't place the same types of demands upon him as they did with others. Lorenzo had established their trust, admiration, and respect. When they reached out to him with their dirty little hands, he embraced them. Lorenzo maintained his commitment to those children for the duration of his time in theater. In his eyes, he was doing whatever he could to improve the lives of innocent children living in harsh conditions. From a higher point of view, Lorenzo was doing God's good work.

Photo by Lorenzo Mulero.

When my first assignment in Kabul ended, I was transferred to Kandahar Airfield (KAF). I was encouraged by the opportunity, because it provided me with a chance to continue developing a professional relationship with my employer; my hope was to gain an extended contract. Moving to KAF meant saying farewell to Lorenzo. I didn't realize it at the time, but parting company with my pal would have a greater impact on me than I could have imagined. When I moved to KAF, I was alone again, living a quiet life while adjusting to other challenges, like the heat, the dust, and the nightly rocket attacks. Kandahar was in the heart of the "big war," as we used to say, where the Taliban and the insurgency were engaged in nonstop battles with the US and our coalition forces. Our enemies gave back as much as they received.

Several months later, I returned to KAIA aboard a C-130. As I disembarked, I looked around my old stomping grounds, taking in the familiar scenery. Ten months earlier, when I had first arrived in Afghanistan as a civilian contractor, I had felt lucky for the opportunity to serve on that dilapidated base; it was the beginning of a new career. On that day, however, I was on my way to bigger and better opportunities. I felt proud. I saw myself as salty veteran from KAF and was rather full of myself. As I approached the NATO offices I ran into my old friend Lorenzo.

"Kevin! You're back!" Lorenzo yelled, throwing up his arms.

We embraced like two brothers who hadn't seen each other in years. I wasn't prepared for the feeling that overcame me; I had a hard time holding back tears. As I reflect on that moment, I realize now that Lorenzo had taken the place of everything that was missing in my life; he had become the family that I longed to be with.

"Jeez, Lorenzo..." Realizing I was caught up in the moment, I took a deep breath to regain my composure. "I really missed you, buddy."

"I missed you, too, you crybaby," he sniffed. "Come on, let's go eat."

Lorenzo's presence seemed to defy everything that was ugly and sad about Afghanistan—and the effect that he had on me was not unique. He was admired by all. The challenges everyone endured, while living in such close quarters—the periodic rocket attacks, the snow, the mud, and the discomfort—dampened people's spirits. To be recognized by so many people as a person of such fine character was nothing short of extraordinary. To be acknowledged by Lorenzo as his friend was even better.

CHAPTER FIVE

The Land of Not Quite Right

The majority of contractors who served in Afghanistan lived and worked within the perimeter fence of a military installation, a condition known as being *inside the wire*. Some of them arrived by convoy while others flew in by commercial and/or military aircraft. Percentagewise, most of the civilian workforce never saw more than what little could be viewed through a chain-link fence. For those of us with jobs that required us to venture outside the wire (in aircraft, automobiles, and tactical vehicles, etc.), we were exposed to sights, sounds, and smells unlike anything we'd experienced.

During my first assignment, I was stationed on KAIA, in Kabul, where I had two construction projects to monitor and a third at the International Security Assistance Force headquarters known as HQ ISAF. The distance between KAIA and HQ ISAF wasn't far, around five kilometers, and for the most part it wasn't a dangerous section of highway—not compared to the road trips that the contractors and combatants made along the streets of Baghdad—which I've been told were a gauntlet of hazards that included IEDs (improvised explosive devices) followed by ambushes. Nevertheless, and depending on a number of variables that included heavy traffic and police checkpoints, the commute could take longer. Every time my colleagues and

I left the safety of a military installation, whether we riding within an armed convoy or a soft vehicle, we felt vulnerable. The sensation of security provided by guard towers, guns, and concertina was gone, baby gone. As we left the base, that big gate slid shut and we were basically on our own—every man for himself. Beyond the danger, the world outside the wire was so full of unusual and often shocking images that newcomers to Afghanistan were astonished by what they saw. The streets outside of KAIA were a portrait of poverty and filth and the roadway was so inundated with deep holes that motorists routinely made wide turns into oncoming lanes to avoid dropping into the voids and losing their forward progress.

Driving in Afghanistan wasn't for the faint of heart and one of the most important rules of the road was to keep moving so you wouldn't get stuck in traffic. This was especially important to Americans who weren't eager to become sitting ducks in a sea of vehicles that could be occupied by potential adversaries and/or vehicle-borne improvised explosive devices known as VBIEDs. The locals, most of whom were cognizant of the threat associated with driving next to a potential target, appeared motivated to be at the head of whatever line they happened to be in. I described this passive-aggressive phenomenon as the "me first" mentality. Whether they were pushing toward the front of the line at the airport check-in or negotiating a roundabout in traffic, the Afghans had this odd proclivity for insisting they be at the front of the line.

Photo by Lorenzo Mulero

Along Kabul's crowded streets, vendors sold everything from produce to used tires, used clothing, and cheap sunglasses. Most of the merchants sold their goods from makeshift kiosks, while others operated from storefronts built from whatever materials could be scavenged. The butcher shops were a sight to behold, and I'm being polite, here—they were actually quite disgusting. The proprietors would slaughter their fowl and livestock out on the street and then hang the cuts of raw meat out in the open air. Flies would feast upon the exposed meat and be shooed away whenever a customer appeared interested. Upon seeing this rather gory and unsanitary venue, one of my fellow American travelers quipped that the *five-second rule* had been modified to accommodate the spirit of the Afghan open market. The practice of employing sarcasm as a way to diffuse the bizarre and repulsive was common.

Photo by Lorenzo Mulero

Public sanitation didn't get much attention in Afghanistan. Raw sewage flowed along the concrete canals between the sidewalk and the streets and vendors set up their display tables in the mud. Garbage trucks would dump their loads in the middle of the city while herds of goats and sheep being led to market competed with the impoverished locals for whatever looked reasonably consumable. Bearing witness to such sights was a bit of a culture shock to those who hadn't seen it before. Newcomers to Afghanistan tended to be taken aback when they witnessed such sights for the first time, but like everything in life, they got used to it. War is hell.

Not all of Afghanistan's people lived in such squalor, but the impressions made by these odd encounters were eye-opening and the basis on which harsh stereotypes took root. The mountains of trash, stagnant water, raw sewage, and public animal slaughter painted an unsightly portrait of what the local citizenry accepted as normal. Sadly, as I learned more about the country and the challenges it either dealt with or ignored, my dismal opinions grew worse.

From the 1930s to the mid-1970s, Kabul was considered the Paris of Central Asia. It was a bustling city with public transportation, beautiful parks, and lush gardens. The women who attended university wore miniskirts. During the reign of the Taliban, females who were accused (and not necessarily guilty) of inappropriate and/or brazen behavior were stoned to death in public. In 1978, Afghanistan's president Sardar Mohammad Daoud Khan was assassinated during a communist coup, and thirty years of war followed. Today, Kabul is recognized as little more than a dilapidated, polluted city that has only moved backward, in terms of political and social progress. Corruption and overpopulation are strangling what was once the country's viable capital, run by a democratic government.

During my first assignment I learned that Kabul's antiquated power grid couldn't support more than a quarter of the city's electrical needs, despite the fact that US taxpayers paid over $300 million for a new power plant. To alleviate Kabul's daily power deficit, gasoline- and diesel-powered generators operate throughout the city. Smoke and exhaust fumes from millions of cars using low-grade fuel produce toxic emissions that claim the lives of 3,000 citizens per year. Fires to heat people's homes produce smoke that pollutes the air, and the practice of burning dried feces to offset the high cost of scarce firewood is common. Prior to the Soviet invasion, Afghanistan was blanketed by approximately 27 million acres of forest, but by the war's end, the

Russians had depleted most of the timber. Today, only 2.5 million acres of forest remain, hence the wood shortage and the need to find creative ways to heat the average inhabitant's uninsulated mud hut. Oddly enough, substituting dry fecal matter for unavailable firewood is common throughout Southwest Asia.

To my surprise, and according to an article written by the US Army Center for Health Promotion and Preventative Medicine, published in March 2004, breathing smoke produced from dry feces (animal or human) doesn't put a person at risk of serious illness. Having grown up in Los Angeles I'm certainly no stranger to air pollution, but the thought of breathing toxic levels of dust, smoke, carbon monoxide, and dried people poop never sat well with me. During my first tour of duty I contracted the flu virus every three to four months. Sometimes I'd be bedridden for days, which seemed odd, because I'd been healthy throughout the vast majority of my life. Contractors and warfighters referred to this condition as the "Kabul Crud."

In an attempt to make light of our peculiar surroundings, I popularized a phrase that I overheard in describing Afghanistan as "The Land of Not Quite Right." Everyone who heard the phrase seemed to connect with its simplistic yet provocative summary. The list of bizarre and recurring events that unfolded daily was a reminder that the world we lived in was weird.

As the war progressed, so too did the political strategies for achieving subsequent objectives, one of which included helping to create a democratic Afghan society. On paper, the strategy of eradicating the Taliban, while simultaneously trying to remold the Afghan culture into a productive, self-sufficient society might have appeared sound, even noble—but in practice it failed. Afghanistan's archaic culture is hindered by centuries of territorial governance known as tribal law. The local inhabitants' limited exposure to how most civilized societies function posed a problem. The introduction of social evolution and nation-building were as peculiar to the local Afghans as climbing Mount Everest while wearing a bathing suit and flippers. Subsequently, the War on Terror, which started out trying to destroy those who sought to promote radical Islamic ideals, evolved into yet another campaign to accomplish what countless armies over the centuries had failed to achieve: control over an uncontrollable region.

In the midst of the war, Afghanistan's survivalist society found opportunity. Commercial business boomed while ignorant bystanders received benefits like manna from heaven. Fresh water wells were dug, schools were built, and food and medicine were distributed generously. Being the experienced and well-versed society that has endured countless conflicts in the past, the Afghan people understood that the rivers of good fortune would not flow forever. As the humanitarian and infrastructure improvements started arriving, therefore, the locals weren't exactly shy about accepting whatever was offered. Were they appreciative? I suppose, but the phrases *Thank you, You're far too kind,* and *How can we ever repay you?* were rarely uttered. One might speculate that the idea of receiving something for nothing was simply too overwhelming for the Afghans to comprehend, but most of the troops and contractors I worked with believed otherwise. We could see that the average Afghan, while quiet and humble, was clever. Experience had taught us that the Afghan people viewed our benevolence as a surplus of whatever we didn't need. How did we arrive at such a biased and harsh conclusion? By witnessing the population's irrepressible demand for *more*—without exerting any effort to reciprocate or demonstrate the capacity to capitalize upon whatever resources were being distributed.

In their defense, the Afghans weren't conscious of their deficiencies. They didn't have the experience to recognize the long-term value of what others were providing. What occurred was no different from a perpetually unemployed welfare recipient who hits the million-dollar lottery and enjoys only a brief period of prosperity before squandering their unexpected fortune. Beyond their own ignorance, however, the Afghan people were certainly wary of their benefactor's ulterior motives. Any nation that spent billions trying to improve Afghanistan's infrastructure while simultaneously bombing selected targets into oblivion surely had something up its sleeve. Consequently,

most of the value of what America and its coalition partners were trying to provide, whether it was first aid, community services, personal
possessions, or the infrastructure to improve quality of life, was consumed quickly and largely unappreciated.

Those of us who witnessed this peculiar exchange failed to embrace its logic. Hundreds of billions of dollars were bestowed upon
a nation that consumed and destroyed resources faster than it was
capable of comprehending why they were receiving them in the first
place. From the perspective of the warfighters and contractors on the
ground, we didn't understand what the politicians were thinking, we
were stupefied: there we were, thousands of miles from home, en-
deavoring to support a cause that provided benefits to a society that
overwhelmingly disapproved of our presence. Taxpayer dollars were
been being dispensed to people who were either turning a blind eye
while our adversaries took measures against us, or actively engaged in
trying to kill us. *Whiskey, Tango, Foxtrot?*

The realization of this absurdity brought to mind one of my favorite quotes: *No good deed goes unpunished.* When I look back on the
investment that was made in Afghanistan and compare it to the number of American and coalition lives lost, I can't help but think that the
returns were minimal at best. The ends did not justify the means.

Several years into my Afghanistan tenure, I resigned from the
NATO agency and teamed up with a Turkish construction company.
The company, whose name shall remain anonymous (they're very
humble and quite well known without any help from my little paint-
by-numbers parable), were rock stars in the world of military construction. Beyond successfully completing over a billion dollars of
strategic enhancements in support of Operation Enduring Freedom
(they accomplished even more during Operation Iraqi Freedom), the
Turks were well known for consistently delivering on-time, quality
projects. To be asked to serve as their Afghanistan business development manager was an honor and a privilege.

The US government routinely leveraged its heavily worded contracts with companies who were hoping to earn profits and willing

to do almost anything for the opportunity for more work. The Turks, being astute businesspeople, understood this and made every diplomatic effort to reduce their losses. As a California building contractor, I was a seasoned veteran of cutthroat business tactics and construction contract warfare. My job description included protecting the Turks' contractual interests, which wasn't a problem: English is a language I happen to read and comprehend quite well. As a result, my association with the Turks turned the tables on a number of cases whereby literally millions of dollars were protected, collected, and/or retrieved.

Unlike many of the US firms who contracted for services inside and outside the wire, the Turks did things differently; they were uniquely independent and stubbornly efficient. Our company was self-funded—and they self-performed their contracts, which is to say they subcontracted very few components within the matrices of their multifaceted projects. We hired local Afghans to assist us in every capacity. We had our own (registered) security division that resembled a small army of AK-47-toting commandos. We didn't need to rely on others for our preservation on the battlefield; we protected ourselves.

Photo from author's collection.

We employed cooks, custodial crews, and driver/escorts to assist in our day-to-day operations. We also hired local commerce agents to assist in purchasing construction materials from the local economy. Our executive branch liaised with government officials and did their bidding with tribal leaders who governed the territories (many of which were hostile) where we were building. By spreading their resources, the Turks were afforded a level of security that reduced the risks associated with doing business in the war zone.

I was the only American within the Turks' 1,500-man Afghanistan contingent and it was comforting to know that my company was extending every effort to ensure my safety. The locals (with whom we did business) knew me, the government officials who visited our headquarters knew me, and across the broad spectrum of our multi-million-dollar operation, I received smiles, handshakes, and respect from people I didn't even know. In retrospect, and when I consider all the business we did within numerous hostile territories—along with the relative ease with which I was able to travel within them—I believe that I was being looked after by people and organizations, who, under other circumstances, would have turned a blind eye to the mayhem taking place on their home turf.

As I alluded to earlier, the nature of my job meant traveling throughout Afghanistan. Much of this time was spent outside the wire where I gained an overall perspective that few contractors were privileged to receive. Sometimes I traveled by commercial aircraft and other times I flew by MILAIR, military air transport. Because of the drug deals they had negotiated with the locals (no pun intended) the Turks felt comfortable tooling around the country in soft (unarmored) vehicles. They didn't own any vehicles that were up-armored; the objective was to blend in with the locals. The Turks were certainly conscious of the risks associated with working in the war zone, but through commerce and trade with the locals they were able to reduce their exposure to hostilities.

I routinely embarked on road trips across the Afghan countryside. Some of the time I traveled with the country manager and our driver, Shadullah, while other times I simply jumped in my SUV and let fate be my guide. When I drove alone, sometimes I was unarmed and other times I carried one or more weapons. Our security company had an armory and as a veteran of the US military the Turks felt comfortable allowing me to draw weapons and ammo to protect myself and my colleagues. Several of my US construction company associates knew I was driving alone and thought I was crazy. Their contracts prohibited them from even venturing outside the wire so it was hard for them to fathom why I took such risks. People would ask me if I ever felt afraid while driving alone, whereby I would reply, "Hell yes." The part I didn't explain was that I also felt confident. Having traveled with numerous escorts and local merchants, I gained a level of insight that enabled me to take calculated risks that most people would never consider. My journeys were preplanned, rarely spontaneous, and only a limited number of people knew where I was going, or when I would be traveling. No one was lying in wait for a lone American driving through the city or along the highway. Indeed, I had some close calls (which you'll read about later) but nothing that dissuaded me from continuing to do what I felt needed to be done. When I needed to get somewhere—and I felt comfortable with the risks—I drove.

Driving through the countryside was an experience that could be disconcerting and entertaining, from one minute to the next. The roadways of Afghanistan were littered with the carcasses of vehicles

Photo from author's collection.

that had been ambushed for their cargo or simply destroyed as yet another target of opportunity for the enemy to exploit. Occasionally, I would happen upon huge craters in the road where IEDs had been deployed. Seeing those reminders that death could come in an instant was equivalent to a drinking a shot of espresso; I felt energized to the point of increasing my awareness of everything around me. On occasion, I simply stopped traveling alone entirely so as not to become complacent.

On the lighter side of traveling through the Land of Not Quite Right, I found many examples that brought either a smile to my face or the occasional "You've gotta be kidding me." The smiles came from seeing little boys with shovels along the roads, backfilling potholes with soil in hopes of earning tips from passing motorists. Seeing a woman with a baby at her breast, sitting in the middle of the street, begging for a handout, was an alarming sight—not that there was anything funny about it—but let's face it, it's not the type of thing you see every day.

I remember seeing a small four-door sedan racing down the highway, packed with seven or eight people crammed inside. They must have had a big family, because three small children were also seated in the open trunk. You would think this would have compelled the driver to operate his vehicle more slowly, but I didn't see any evidence

Photo by Larry Currid

of it. Every time the car hit a bump, the kids would hit their heads on the open trunk and laugh. After capturing that Kodak moment on my cell phone, I overtook the sedan so I wouldn't have to witness the aftermath of whatever tragedy might ensue.

Afghanistan doesn't employ state troopers to patrol its roadways so the enforcement of highway safety is virtually nonexistent. Transport trucks were routinely overladen with cargo to the point of tipping over. Forty-foot containers were placed on twenty-foot flatbed trucks, whose front tires could barely maintain contact with the road. If a two-lane city street could accommodate three vehicles abreast, then that two-lane roadway became a six-lane thoroughfare. Oftentimes, a tractor-trailer rig driving along one of the outer lanes would cut off both directions of traffic while executing a U-turn.

One afternoon, I was driving alone from Bagram to Kabul on Jalalabad Road. I had just entered the city limits and was transiting through a commercial area where thousands of shipping containers were stored. The two-lane highway had a wide shoulder on both sides with tractor-trailer rigs parked two and three abreast. Along the shoulder, trucks were being loaded and unloaded, while their drivers were either performing maintenance or resting in their cabs. It was a busy section of town, but one I was I familiar with.

As I was driving down the road, minding my own business, a pickup truck carrying a group of locals, brandishing AK-47s and RPGs (rocket-propelled grenade launchers), cut me off as it swerved onto the highway. My speed was approximately sixty kilometers per hour, and beyond the surprise of the rapidly merging vehicle was the fact that sitting in the back of the pickup were blanket-wearing locals with enough firepower to start a small war. I decelerated slowly, trying to put some distance between our two vehicles without drawing attention. Visions of being forced off the road or getting into a gunfight flickered through my head. As an American, I knew I'd make a good hostage, or a subject for exploitation over the internet. I glanced at the AK-47 I had placed along the kick-panel next to my left foot, touched the crucifix beneath my shirt, and said a quick prayer. From that point forward, everything seemed to move in slow motion.

My mind was racing, but the images in my subconscious appeared clearly, as if I had minutes to observe each frame. Fortunately, I managed to keep my cool. I was scared, but I didn't panic. I correctly calculated that if I were the target of these road warriors, they would have pulled alongside me, sprayed my car with bullets, or forced me to pull over. Checking my rearview mirror, I noted the angle of the dirt road from which their vehicle had entered the highway. The driver, who was probably amped-up on adrenaline, opium, or the excitement of the jihad he and his buddies were about to embark upon had probably failed to look for any merging traffic.

These guys aren't interested in me, I concluded. *This whole thing is nothing more than a coincidence.*

My accelerated heart rate posed the only real threat that existed that day, for within seconds of entering my line of sight the truck in front of me sped away. The assailants appeared to be late for an appointment, and I was only too glad that said appointment wasn't with me. Just to be sure, I made a casual left turn onto a paved side street and headed in the opposite direction.

After five minutes of checking my rearview mirror, I started breathing again. My stomach was in knots, so I grabbed the one-liter bottle of water on the passenger seat and chugged until I choked.

Along that same busy road, several years later, I was driving at a fairly good pace while en route to my camp near the Kabul international airport. As always, there was a flurry of activity on both sides of the highway. To avoid drawing any attention to the fact I was alone (and an American) I maintained my speed, mirroring the flow of traffic in front of me, which as always was clicking along at a pace that was well above the safety factor for a commercial area. From the corner of my eye, I could see several young boys chasing a dog, throwing rocks and waving a stick to alter its direction as it ran away from them. At the last second, the dog darted right in front of my vehicle while the boys stopped short of the highway and watched. By the look on the boys' faces I could see they had intended to do exactly what was transpiring: they had forced the dog to run onto the highway—right in front of my vehicle.

I had heard stories about local kids forcing dogs and cats to run out into the street, whereby the animals would get run over while the onlookers watched. It was a sick form of entertainment, but life was cheap in the Land of Not Quite Right, especially for homeless and unwanted animals. I had heard cases where expat drivers had stopped their vehicles to see if the animal they had struck was injured. Upon exiting their vehicles, the animal-chasers would initiate a con game whereby they'd play-act and become boisterous in an attempt to extort money from their unsuspecting prey.

As the dog veered into my rapidly approaching vehicle I realized that an impact was imminent. Without hesitating, I gripped the wheel, released my foot from the accelerator, and continued steering straight ahead. Trying to avoid the animal by swerving or slamming on the brakes might have compromised my position; I couldn't afford to lose control of the vehicle or put myself in danger. The dog, which I could see as it darted in front of my car, was no more than a puppy. The dog made it past my right front tire, but I felt a slight shudder in the steering wheel as the left front tire made contact. Over the whine of my off-road tires I heard a distinct yelp of pain. I winced with regret but forced myself not to overreact and remained calm. I wasn't about to pull over, or even appear as though I was aware the incident had occurred. Without slowing down, I proceeded down the highway as if nothing had happened.

From my side mirror, I saw the dog tumble and recover. As I began to accelerate, I watched the scene unfolding in the rearview mirror. I couldn't hear the activity behind me, but I could see that the dog was yelping in pain as it limped off the highway, favoring what looked to be either a broken back leg or a crushed hip. As the image of the injured dog disappeared from view I realized that nothing would come of the incident. No sooner had it happened than it had been forgotten by anyone who had witnessed the event, everyone except me.

Several minutes later, the reality of what had just occurred began to register: I'd hit a dog with my car and I didn't even try to avoid it. Making matters worse, I knew the dog was only a puppy, six to eight months old, perhaps. I felt certain it wouldn't survive such a trauma, not in Afghanistan. Try as I might, I could not dismiss the episode as a justifiable action for ensuring my own safety. I couldn't block the vision I'd seen through the side mirror, nor silence the painful cry I'd heard. I don't know if I was experiencing rage or sadness, perhaps it was both, but tears welled up in my eyes and my throat tightened as I fought to hold back my emotions. I felt overcome by a sensation of helplessness and despair. I didn't cry, but instead I cursed, and screamed, and hit the dashboard so hard I nearly broke my hand.

Perhaps for the sake of my own sanity, I repressed the memory of that day for many years. Until composing my thoughts for this chapter, I'd forgotten all about it, or so I thought. I can still see the three boys chasing the dog: one of them had thrown a rock that skipped across the pavement in front of me. Another boy had a long stick that he flailed while his companion followed in glee. The look on their faces was that of children who could have been chasing the ice cream man down the street.

I'll never understand such levels of ignorance and cruelty. Had I crushed the dog beneath my tires and killed it outright, I might have felt relief. The outcome would have been quick; no suffering would have been allowed. That's not the way it played out, however, and for that (too) I felt terrible.

While in Afghanistan, I somehow managed to forget that that terrible day. Now I regret ever remembering it. I don't regret doing what I had to, but to this day I'm still moved to tears while remembering every vivid detail. It's a hell of a thing.

CHAPTER SIX

A Day in the Life

After a while, the road trips outside the wire were uneventful, despite the fact that nothing had changed: the living conditions throughout Kabul and its surrounding areas were unsanitary, traffic was chaotic, and the presence of military convoys rumbling through the streets was common. For the average American, this certainly wasn't the type of scene one might expect to find back home, but in Kabul, it was par for the course.

While on leave in the US, my sister Susan asked me the $65,000 question: "What's it like over there? Aren't you scared?"

I hesitated in responding because it felt awkward admitting that I'd grown accustomed to living in such a harsh environment. I had encountered so many episodes of sadness and misery that life in a war zone seemed normal. Unless you've been exposed to that type of environment, it's difficult to articulate, let alone comprehend how people can become oblivious to it—but it happens; human beings are an adaptable species. With that in mind, I thought it would be interesting to read about one of my typical days in Afghanistan. As a preface to this *story within a story* I'd like to note that most contractors didn't have the chance (nor desire) to do some of the things I did. By the same token, I'm sure there were many who experienced challenges that were more dangerous and interesting. Nevertheless, here's an excerpt from one of my average days.

The clock next to my bed read 4:12 a.m. Like every other morning, I awoke several minutes ahead of the alarm. My day wasn't set to begin for another three hours, but I needed exercise if I hoped to stay in shape. My average weight was around 230 pounds, but at 6'2" I was both tall and muscular, and managed the weight with little difficulty. As an early riser, I could expect to run out of gas by 9:00 p.m., and the morning workout provided me with a boost of endorphins that energized me throughout the day.

My gym clothes were on the dresser, where I had placed them neatly the night before: tighty-whitey Hanes briefs, Under Armour gym shorts, and one of the several souvenir T-shirts I had purchased at the post exchange. Sitting neatly on the floor was a $250 pair of New Balance cross-trainers with a clean pair of white socks folded inside. I admit to having spent too much for workout sneakers, but I didn't have many luxuries back then so I treated myself from time to time. After getting dressed, I jumped into my SUV and drove to the gym on KAIA. By 7:30, I had completed my cardio and weightlifting program, eaten breakfast, showered, dressed, and was ready to begin a new day.

The living accommodations within our camp were well appointed. My employers (the Turks) had built a ten-acre facility that was lush with gardens, an expansive water feature, and shade trees that took the edge off of living in the midst of one of Kabul's average neighborhoods, a filthy ghetto. To mitigate the possibility of unauthorized persons entering our compound, the Turks constructed a twelve-foot rock wall that encircled the perimeter. On top of the wall were coils of concertina wire and the entrance to our facility was secured by a one-inch-thick steel gate. Our company had its own government-registered security division that employed dozens of local nationals who were trained and supervised by a former member of the Turkish special forces. The security guards were well disciplined, respectful, and armed. Most of them were bearded, and some appeared undernourished, but none were unkempt in appearance; everyone was outfitted in a clean uniform, combat boots, and a matching baseball cap displaying the company logo. Some of the men tried to look like commandos, which was reassuring, but the gear they were wearing seemed to fall short of providing any utility; the extra ammo pouches were empty and the Kevlar plates were missing from their bulletproof vests. There was one aspect of authenticity that couldn't be discounted, however, and that was the Kalashnikov rifles they were carrying. Did they know how to use them? I had no way of knowing—and I hoped I would never have to find out.

Maintaining our little world required a fair amount of effort and my employers spared no expense. We produced our own electricity with two locomotive-sized diesel-powered generators and drilled a pair of deep-water wells to supply the camp with fresh water that was plentiful and sweet. Feeding our 800-man construction crew was facilitated by a commercial kitchen and a staff of more than a dozen cooks and helpers. There was a laundry facility, a custodial crew to keep our offices and living quarters clean and tidy, and a doctor who resided on the premises. We had a 2,500-square-foot recreation room with sofas, TV, pool tables, card tables, and a bar, though alcohol wasn't served every night and excessive drinking was frowned upon.

Within the compound were concrete-hardened living quarters and warehouses for storing tools and equipment. We had a carpenter's shop, a welding shop, and a parking lot full of construction equipment and building materials valued at millions of dollars. Visitors who stopped by to conduct business were not only impressed by our operation, they marveled at its cleanliness. The size and scale of our construction company required at least a dozen or more administrators. With a country manager at the helm, we had accountants, procurement agents, contracting officers, and local business managers who carried out their work from an office building that rivaled the volume of activity you'd expect to find at an assembly plant.

After my shower, I headed to my private office to review whatever email traffic had transpired in the night before. Aziz, whose job was to provide tea and coffee to the office staff throughout the day, entered my office with a cup of Nescafé.

"Good morning, Mr. Kevin," Aziz said with a tight-lipped smile. He was more concerned about spilling my coffee than saying hello. Beneath the cup he placed a folded Kleenex tissue.

"Thank you, Aziz," I replied without lifting my eyes from the laptop. My hand instinctively moved to where he placed the cup every morning. I blew into the cup and took a sip. It was too hot to drink, so I let it cool. Minutes later, I realized I had become preoccupied reading emails and had missed that point where the coffee could be enjoyed most: a tad bit hot, but not so hot that you can't taste the flavor. Had I opted for a fresh cup, Aziz would have accommodated my request, but on that morning, I didn't have time; I was anxious to get going.

After banging out a few email responses, I grabbed my laptop and headed out the door. It was still shy of 8:00 a.m. but I had a fair amount of ground to cover along with a list of tasks that I needed to get done.

The first order of business was the commute to one of several projects sites that I was responsible for monitoring. Bagram Airfield was about an hour away, but I wouldn't be flying there; I wasn't going to waste my time sitting at the military PAX (passenger) terminal for three to four hours, not when I could drive the distance in less than a third of the time. The only hook was that I'd have to travel by car across the Wild West; *Indian Country*, as we used to say. Knowing that none of the other managers had any business outside of our headquarters that day, I had a decision to make: I could ask our executive driver (Shadullah), to take me, or drive alone. Having made the trip many times before, I opted to fly solo.

Before jumping into my SUV I went into the accountant's office to pick up some insurance for my solo trip: weapons and ammo. The accountant, Mevlüt (whom I addressed as *Mr. Mevlüt*), unlocked the cabinet and handed me an AK-47, a nine-millimeter pistol, and several extra magazines. Mr. Mevlüt could have been handing me some sticky notes and highlighter pens; it was all the same to him.

"Bah-Gram?" he asked.

Mr. Mevlüt didn't speak a word of English, but I understood him most of the time.

"Yep," I said, stuffing the banana clip magazines in my cargo pockets. "I'm going to Bagram."

I clipped the pistol to my belt. He sat at his desk, folded his hands, and watched me. He said something to me in Turkish that I didn't understand but ended his sentence with a word I recognized: "Inshallah." Mr. Mevlüt was telling me to be careful, and that God willing (*inshallah*), I would be delivered to my destination safely. As I slung the rifle behind my back, I responded with a demonstration I knew he would understand: I pulled the crucifix from beneath my shirt, showed it to him, and replied, "Inshallah." Mevlüt winked.

"Thank you, sir," I said, turning toward to door. "Hope to see you soon," I murmured to myself as I walked down the office hallway. *Inshallah*.

I never took to the streets of Afghanistan without a specific purpose in mind. Afghanistan wasn't the type of place for a Sunday drive. My longest solo trips lasted no more than a couple of hours, whereby I'd drive from Kabul to Bagram Airfield, aka BAF (*baff*), which was approximately forty kilometers (twenty-five miles) north of Kabul. BAF served as a FOB for US and coalition forces. Beyond being home to squadrons of attack helicopters, MEDEVAC (medical evacuation) aerial ambulances, shuttle service aircraft, and several fighter jet squadrons, BAF also served as a strategic way station for supplies that were forwarded to other FOBs and combat outposts known as COPs. BAF was also home to over 35,000 troops and civilian contractors. Our company had a sizeable footprint inside the wire. We had a man camp housing over 600 construction workers supporting over a half-dozen projects valued at over $150 million. The nature of my job required me to spend much of my time on BAF, so the Turks provided me with living quarters, where I kept a separate wardrobe and all the accoutrements of a second home. This enabled me to travel light. All I needed to take with me were my car keys, laptop computer, guns, ammunition, and snacks.

After some last-minute emails, I had a quick meeting with the country manager, Mehmet, to inform him of my departure and destination. No one else was aware of my travel plans because I didn't want anyone waiting for me with his finger on the triggering device of an IED somewhere along the roadway. As I warmed the engine of my Toyota Land Cruiser, I sent a text to my colleague and friend Larry, a retired Navy (Seabee) chief petty officer who worked as a project manager on BAF. Along with Mehmet, Larry was on standby, in case I had a problem along the route between Kabul and Bagram. Larry knew that if he didn't hear from me in three or four hours he was to call Mehmet, who would dispatch a team to come looking for me.

The military neither encouraged nor discouraged such movements across the badlands because they weren't tasked with looking after civilian contractor safety. Moreover, they didn't have the manpower to support all the trips that contractors were required to make outside the wire. To mitigate our risk, contractors were welcome to fly as space-available (Space-A) passengers aboard military aircraft, but the flights were often rescheduled and tended to be time consuming. The show time, or advanced time frame that passengers were required to be at the airport, was several hours prior to departure. Barring a mishap (which rarely occurred) contractors flying Space-A were guaranteed safe passage, but in the case of a flight from Kabul to BAF (which took less than fifteen minutes) I usually opted for the road trip. I had driven the route dozens of times, I understood the risks, and I didn't care to spend much of my day languishing in a passenger terminal. I had work to do.

Once I hit the road, it was business as usual. The cop at the roundabout near the entrance of the Kabul airport recognized me and smiled, which under the circumstances was commendable; traffic that morning was as fierce as ever. Taxi drivers in Cairo couldn't hold a candle to the kamikaze drivers of Kabul. To avoid the possibility of a fender bender I usually surrendered my right-of-way to the locals, who drove as if they were competing in a demolition derby. On occasion, I'd have to swerve my big Toyota SUV in the path of other cars to avoid an accident. The blocking maneuver was an effective way to keep unsafe and persistent drivers at bay. Whenever I employed such radical tactics I'd receive looks of astonishment from the other drivers. Hand gestures would follow, and expletives in Pashto and Dari. *Whatever, dude. Have a nice day.*

Eventually, I broke free of the city's grip and started motoring at greater speeds through Kabul's commercial district on the outskirts of town. This was where I'd hit the dog, about a year earlier, but that memory had been stowed behind a mental firewall to protect me from being distracted. The commercial district was a popular rest stop for the jingle trucks. The term "jingle truck" was coined to describe any freight-carrying rig that was heavily decorated with paintings and ornate metals hanging from the bumpers, which created a melodic jingle as they lumbered down the highway. Every jingle truck had its own unique design scheme; some of them were quite spectacular.

As I cruised through Kabul's commercial district the sea of shipping containers was replaced by rolling hills dotted with two-story houses—substantial properties, by local standards, most of which appeared to have been abandoned during construction. With the change in scenery, traffic began to thin, so I relaxed and let out a sigh of relief. The mild stress level that I'd been concealing came down a few notches. The drive to BAF always started out as stressful, as I never knew what I might get into. Only two people in the world were aware that I was traveling at that moment. I was relatively invisible in my silver SUV, motoring inconspicuously among the locals.

For those of you wondering, *What was this guy thinking—driving alone in Afghanistan?* I'll take a moment to explain where my head was.

I need to go back several decades, to a time when I was in high school. As a sophomore, I had a friend by the name of Tom Fritz. Tom and I were on the swim team together, and he invited me over to his house after school one day. Tom's mother made us sandwiches while Tom and I sat at the table, listening to her questions about my interests and family life. As the questions seemed to probe deeper, she explained that she had an interest in astrology. When Mrs. Fritz asked if I would mind if she did an astrological profile on me, I replied, "Why not? That sounds interesting."

I've always been open-minded. I listen to theories, do a fair amount of reading, and consider myself pragmatic and fair. I've never seen a UFO, but I wouldn't be surprised to learn that there are other species of intelligent life among the billions of stars throughout the universe.

A couple of weeks later, I returned to Tom's house to hang out with my buddy, be treated to another sandwich, and hear the results of his mother's astrological profile on yours truly.

"You'll always be taken care of, Kevin," she said. "You'll experience ups and downs throughout your life, but overall, you're going to be all right; you'll always land on your feet."

I was pleased but not surprised by Mrs. Fritz's assessment. Since I was a young boy I've always had an inner sense that my life would not only turn out to be okay, it would be exceptional. That feeling was also present while I was in Afghanistan. Whenever I found myself feeling afraid, I blocked out whatever was distracting me and focused instead on figuring out what I needed to do to feel better.

About a quarter of the way into my journey was an Afghan checkpoint manned by members of the ANP, the Afghan National Police force. The checkpoint was along Jalalabad Road, or "Route Bottle" as it was called by the US forces that traveled along the section of highway between Kabul and Bagram. As I pulled up to the checkpoint, I checked to see that my AK-47 was snuggled into the floorboard between the door and my left leg. The policeman, standing in the middle of the road, positioned on the left-hand side of the vehicle as I approached the checkpoint, would never see the weapon—not that it would have mattered; most of the cops had seen me carrying a weapon in the past and they didn't care. They knew me as the guy who routinely stuffed five dollars in their hands as I drove by.

On that day, like many days, a pair of police officers checked the vehicles as they passed. These were routine checks, which didn't consist of anything more than a passing glance at the drivers as they were waved through the checkpoint. Rarely would the ANP stop a vehicle with Americans on board; the Afghans didn't speak English. On that day, however, one of the officers signaled to me to stop as I approached the speed bump.

Okay. What does this guy want?

The familiar-looking officer seemed to have something on his mind. With a smile, he pointed up the road and uttered a one-word question that I understood immediately. "Ba-gram?"

"Yes," I replied, "Bagram." *I'm headed to Bagram...now what?*

Pointing to his colleague, the policeman smiled and repeated himself, "Ba-gram!"

Now I get it; this guy wants me to give his buddy a ride. He's probably coming off shift and wants a lift.

After giving the second cop a quick visual inspection, I could see he was rather frail and unarmed. He appeared harmless, so I decided to accommodate him.

"Y'allah," I offered. *Let's go, get in.*

That wasn't the first time I ever gave a ride to an Afghan along the highway, nor would it be my last. Transporting a local national actually served as an advantage: seeing an American driving with an Afghan (let alone a cop) was so rare that whoever happened to notice us would do a double take; they didn't know what to make of it. In effect, it was a great ruse.

Content with having scored a ride home, my travel companion made his way around the front of my vehicle and climbed aboard. Avoiding any uncomfortable outcomes that might have been prompted when he saw the weapons I was carrying, I remained focused on his colleague, who was pumping my hand and thanking me in Dari. "Taşhakür, Taşhakür" (*Thank you! Thank you!*)

With the sweeping motion of his arm, as if presenting me the highway for my sole pleasure, the first policeman beckoned me to proceed. As I accelerated, I shook my head, impressed by what was developing: Not only was I driving alone in a soft vehicle along a highway in Afghanistan, I was now being accompanied by an Afghan policeman who didn't speak a word of English. *You can't make this stuff up.*

As my rather fragrant passenger settled into his seat, he took in his surroundings and noticed the AK-47 on the floorboard next to my left leg. His assessment also revealed that his driver outweighed him by a hundred or more pounds, and there was a pistol clipped to his belt.

I remained nonchalant while he sized me up. Having done the math in his head, my colleague must have equated that getting a ride home superseded whatever risk he may have momentarily contemplated. Satisfied with his inspection, he confirmed the conclusion that he had drawn about me:

"Amerikhan commando?" he asked in his best attempt at English.

"Yes," I replied, not wishing to minimize any advantage I had inadvertently acquired.

"Ho-*kay*," he responded, and with that the inquiry was concluded.

The rest of our journey consisted of hand signals and short phrases that helped me determine that my passenger, Mohamed Jan, lived in the village of Bagram, had two children (genders unknown), and hadn't showered since the Russians invaded back in 1979. A toothbrush might have been a welcome addition to his personal hygiene kit, but I didn't hold it against him; Mohamed was neither pretentious nor ambitious. He was just an average guy—like me, perhaps—with one exception: I had showered that morning and didn't smell like a goat.

As was customary, I'd brought along some Cheetos and a couple of cans of 7-Up for the trip. Mohamed and I shared a snack; we clicked

Photo by Lorenzo Mulero

our cans together like two men toasting their good fortune and crunched on Cheetos until our fingers were stained with that orange, sticky residue. Along the route there were several other checkpoints, but unlike the one where I'd picked up my passenger, these weren't manned by policemen conducting inspections. At most, there was a speed bump to slow down traffic, and alongside the road were ramshackle guardhouses, occupied by one or more lazy officers who appeared to recognize Mohamed. The looks of shock and jealousy on their faces were followed by a guttural laugh from Mohamed, who appeared to derive a degree of pleasure from having gained an advantage over his colleagues. Over the next few checkpoints, Mohamed got cocky by hanging out the window and waving as if to say, *Look at me fellas, I'm riding in style!* Each time he shouted out the window, I smiled and shook my head. I was starting to feel like a chauffeur for a guy who made less money in a year than I earned in less than a week. I nevertheless took pleasure in providing the foundation for a story that Mohamed Jan would share for the rest of his life.

As we drove down the road there were numerous reminders of the dangers that existed on the highway: two burned-out, forty-foot fuel trucks sat rusting on the shoulder. The cabs had been gutted by fire, the tires had melted from the ensuing blaze, and both vehicles were pocked with bullet holes from what must have been an ambush. The fuel cells behind the tractors appeared to have been penetrated by rocket-propelled grenades; the tanks were blown out with shards of metal, twisted in ways that only a massive explosion could have created.

"Taliban," uttered Mohamed Jan, shaking his head in pity. That was all he said, but the way he said it and the expression on his face spoke volumes: the perpetrators of the carnage were not his people.

After another hour passed, Mohamed Jan asked to be dropped on a dirt road that led to his village. Entering Bagram Airfield was as challenging as always; the variety and intensity of vehicle and personnel inspections required more time than the commute itself. The lines of vehicles entering the base were directed into lanes, whereby all the doors, engine compartments, and trunks had to be opened for inspection. The vehicles' occupants were herded into a secure area while bomb-sniffing dogs did their thing. The military police inspected literally hundreds of vehicles per day and were in no hurry. In the wake of their inspections, the K-9s would leave dusty paw prints on the upholstery. *Damn dogs.* After finally being allowed to enter the base the sensation of being inside the wire was almost worth the wait. I stopped checking my rearview mirror and relaxed.

The largest of the forward operating bases functioned like cities. There were fire departments, hospitals, post offices, shopping districts, and residential areas. Like most modern cities, they were designed by a master planner, whose job was to engineer a layout that incorporated security requirements, mission-essential facilities, and the development of an infrastructure that would support both current and future operations. The location of every feature on-base, whether it was the placement of an air traffic control tower along the airfield, or a new Burger King at the food court, was reviewed and approved by the base commander.

The majority of BAF's population were soldiers: ground-pounders and trigger-pullers, many of whom went outside the wire, patrolled the roads, and hunted down the enemy. While armed with a skill set that identified them as specialists in their field, the powers that be didn't always house soldiers along the outer perimeter—which would have made sense, when you consider that if an attack were launched from a neighboring village, like the ones that were within a stone's throw away from the perimeter (and there were several such villages just outside the wire), then the assets needed to deal with the problem would already be in place. Oddly enough, or perhaps by design, most of the warfighters were housed closer to the center of the FOB while the contractor camps encircled the periphery. The civilian contractors living on BAF didn't overlook the fact that they had been placed between the enemy and the troops who were well suited to eliminate such threats, but there was little we could do but laugh and describe ourselves jokingly as the outermost line of the military's unarmed defense.

Two hours after leaving Kabul, I arrived at our man camp, threw my car into park, grabbed my laptop, slung my weapon over my shoulder, and headed for my hooch. While en route, I ran into a colleague named Kurt.

Kurt was about three years my senior, and he had retired from the National Guard as full-bird colonel. Kurt was tall, with nonthreatening blue eyes, and wore his straight, gray hair a little longer than most retirees of his rank and tenure. Kurt had the approachable demeanor of a summer camp counselor. He didn't fit the stereotype of how most people might imagine an Army colonel, but he must have known it, for even after serving in numerous combat campaigns Kurt was mildmannered. He was humble and seemed almost embarrassed by the fact that he'd "been there, done that" more times than he cared to discuss. Veterans recognize this trait as a telltale sign of those who have had exemplary careers.

Kurt worked for an American construction company that served as the prime contractor on the construction projects my employers were supporting. It was an unusual relationship, in that Kurt and his US colleagues didn't always appear to be actually doing anything, much of the time—not that they're weren't; it's only that our crews were doing most of the actual work while Kurt and his team supervised.

Photo from author's collection.

Kurt's company was responsible for making sure that my company was performing to the standards set forth in our US contract, a contract that could blindside even the shrewdest American company—let alone a Turkish company that didn't read *Harvard Law Review* English. From a contractual standpoint, the employees of the prime contractor had positional authority over their Turkish counterparts, but in terms of construction experience, the Turks were certainly capable of executing the work (correctly) without any help.

Among my many responsibilities as the business development manager, I was hired to mitigate problems associated with the cultural challenges that arose between a Turkish company, Kurt's American firm, and our client, the US Government. Overseas contracting could be tricky, and the Turks were not always cognizant of when they weren't meeting customer expectations or being set up for failure. Government contracting is not for the faint of heart (especially in a war zone), and there were those who were known to exploit any advantage that could be gained from the opposing team or partners within their own organizations. The Turks were certainly privy to the pitfalls of a game that promised great rewards to those who were willing to take risks, but the process of achieving that objective required assistance from time to time, and that's where I came in.

Armed with the experience the Turks needed me to provide, I routinely averted contractually unjust conditions that Kurt's company and/or the USG were trying to impose. As a result, I was resented by certain individuals who were prone to trying to take advantage of my employer's naïveté and reluctance to upset their clients. Using me, their American buffer, served the Turks' interests. It limited their exposure without their having to take the blame for rocking the boat with their customers.

"I see you made it back safely from another trip out there in the wild, wild west!" Kurt chuckled.

"How's it going, Kurt?" I asked, greeting him with a firm handshake.

"I'm living the dream, brother, you know how it is."

"You ought to come with me sometime, Kurt. You'd like it out there."

"I'd love to!" he said, laughing. "My company might get a little freaked out, however, so we'll have to make it a *covert* mission."

The rules that governed Kurt's movements, in and outside the wire, were clearly defined by an employment contract, written by a staff of corporate lawyers who spent weeks preparing an ironclad, litigation-proof document that would defend Kurt's company from any claims of compensation resulting from injuries or death sustained in the combat zone. My contract with the Turks was less elaborate; it directed me to represent their interests in a moral and professional manner in exchange for a handsome salary—plus a percentage bonus for every new job I helped them acquire. I didn't worry about violating company security protocols, because there weren't any. My company did what it had to do in order to survive in Afghanistan and make money. As a result of having agreed to such terms, Kurt and some of his associates viewed me as something of a cowboy. At risk of sounding brash (and I know I tend to), I wore that distinction as a badge of honor.

After stowing my gear in my hooch (living container), I headed straight for Larry's office; I needed to tell him I had arrived safely. Larry lived and worked out of a forty-foot converted sea container that served as an office/sleeping quarters. Larry's accommodations were what was called a *wet unit,* a fully self-contained housing unit that included a toilet, sink, and shower. It was a sweet setup, whereby Larry could wake up in the morning, walk ten feet from his bedroom to take a shower, get dressed, and be in his office without ever setting foot outside.

After knocking twice, I let myself into the office section of Larry's trailer.

"Honey, I'm home!"

"Right on," Larry replied. That was his way of acknowledging he could forget thinking about me traveling across the desert alone in my SUV. Now that I had arrived safely, Larry was off the hook.

Larry and I had worked together for several years. We were both friends and professional colleagues who served in the US Navy Seabees as chief petty officers—brothers from another mother, so to speak.

Larry offered me a cup of coffee as we settled in for some chitchat. Like all Genuine Chief Petty Officers, Larry had a hot pot of coffee available throughout all hours of the day. Next to the coffeemaker were several clean mugs hanging from a rack. There were stir sticks, a sugar dispenser, fresh milk in the minifridge, and a tin full of imported Danish butter cookies. I took two.

I used to joke with Larry by describing him as the war zone's Martha Stewart. Everything in his office was clean, perfectly arranged, and comfy as a vacation cottage. As I looked around, I was reminded that this was not only where Larry spent most of his time, it was reflection his personality. Like most of the civilian workforce in Afghanistan, Larry was a patriot. There was a small American flag in a coffee mug that served as a pen and pencil holder on his desk, photos of picturesque American landscapes on the walls, college football banners, and other miscellaneous souvenirs on display. Larry's office was a menagerie of paraphernalia that had been carefully organized so as to provide a reminder to himself and his visitors that there was more to him than met the eye.

Mr. Larry (as his workers called him) was also an avid reader. He liked to keep abreast of current affairs and was an amateur history buff. Spending time with Larry was not only a pleasure; it was an opportunity to share knowledge and learn something new. Larry's affable personality also gained him access to a lot of intel on the FOB from key people in positions of influence up and down the military's chain of command. Thanks to his people skills, he was affiliated with a number of social and professional circles inside the wire. Larry was well connected.

As I sipped on my coffee, Larry leaned back in his chair and provided me with the details of the latest rocket attacks, force protection changes, speed traps, parking space enforcement, and an update of all the new merchandise that had arrived at the PX. Larry was a bank vault of information, but he wasn't a blabbermouth. Knowledge was wealth within our world, and information was currency.

After the unofficial brief was complete, Larry shifted gears and began talking about the status of his projects. As always, he had things under control, so I thanked him for the coffee, excused myself, and headed to my office. After checking in with the site project manager, I jumped back into my Toyota to conduct some jobsite inspections. The rest of the day was uneventful, just the way I liked it. While checking on the status of our projects, I shook hands with the workers, thanked them for a job well done, and joked with the Air Force escorts who were shadowing our work force as they constructed improvements along the airfield.

At our camp dining facility, that evening, I reconnected with Larry, who was accompanied by three women from the Air Force he had invited to dinner.

Good old Larry. Dude hasn't lost his touch.

After dinner, I went to my office for a final check of emails before turning in for the evening. By 8:30, I was showered and already in bed. Like my other accommodation in Kabul, my bedroom on BAF was modest, with a few touches of home: photos of my children stapled to the drywall, and a snapshot of my wife and me in Paris—memories of a life that that didn't exist in the Land of Not Quite Right, but one I hoped to see again.

I can't recall what I had done all day, it didn't seem like much, but I remember feeling exhausted. Driving alone across the Afghan desert had a way of sapping my energy. My attention was on high alert throughout the drive, and it felt as though I were a fugitive on the run from a pack of hounds.

As I did every night, I read a little before turning off the light, and within five minutes I was sleeping like a baby. Sometime during the night, I heard the distinctive sound of a reverberating concussion, a double-tap: *boom boom.* Having heard that sound so many times before, I knew what was happening: *incoming rounds.* We were being attacked.

As the sirens began to wail in the distance, I could hear the airbase being awakened and ordered into bunkers. Giant loudspeakers dispersed throughout the FOB blared their audible instructions: "Indirect fire, don IBA and proceed to a protective shelter." The announcement from the loudspeakers (known as the Giant Voice system) was repeated for several minutes. "Indirect fire, don IBA and proceed to a protective shelter."

Despite all the ruckus, I didn't move from beneath my covers. I hadn't even opened my eyes. By the sound of the explosion, I could calculate where the rocket had hit—on the other side of the base. Within seconds, I had fallen back asleep.

My good buddy, Lorenzo, had a gift for making everyone smile.
Photo by Lorenzo Mulero

Aircraft parking apron construction/expansion efforts were
among some of the many projects that I participated in. *Photo
from author's collection.*

Larry Currid was a good colleague who always had a fresh pot of coffee and cookies for whoever dropped by his field office. Larry is standing next to a Jingle Truck. *Photo by Larry Currid*

Barbara and I during a dinner celebration for newly promoted US Navy Chief Petty Officers. Promoting the rank of CPO was one of the proudest days of my life. *Photo from author's collection.*

Construction projects on the edge of an active runway required work crews to be only meters away from departing and arriving aircraft. The armed USAF escort's job was to keep an eye on the workforce. *Photo from author's collection.*

The Burbs: B-Huts made of plywood slept up to eight people in little cubicles that provided privacy for the occupants, and enough space to stow their gear. *Photo from author's collection.*

My B-Hut accommodations were comfortable yet without the
benefit of bathroom, which was located over 100-yards away.
Photo from author's collection.

Civilian contractors were routinely afforded transportation
aboard US Army Blackhawk helicopters. Flying without my body
armor suggests that this photo was taken during the earlier years
of the war. *Photo from author's collection.*

Barbara and I were fond of vacationing in Egypt while I was working downrange. *Photo from author's collection.*

LtCol Kevin Cullen, USAF (left) poses with me, at Camp Cunningham on BAF. When I learned that there was another Kevin Cullen serving in Afghanistan, I sent the LtCol an email to which he replied, "Get over here, let's meet!" *Photo from author's collection.*

Transportation to and from dangerous jobsites in Afghanistan was provided by helicopter. A good friend of mine, Ron Francis, was a project manager in the hostile province of Ghazni. *Photo from author's collection.*

Blu Burch (left) and Dave Russell were a pair of highly-skilled builders who left their homes in Utah to help the war effort. Blu and Dave could always be counted on to do whatever needed to be done. *Photo from author's collection.*

Cursed by the Cat

Habibiti (*ha-be-be-tee*—*Arabic: sweetheart [female]*) was a feral cat born on the streets of Al Mahooz in the Kingdom of Bahrain. Just prior to working as a civilian contractor, I was on active duty in Bahrain, home to the US Navy's Fifth Fleet. Naval Support Activity (NSA) Bahrain didn't include base housing for most of the sailors who were stationed there. Instead, the government provided funds to their men and women in uniform, to rent flats and villas (apartments and houses) out on the local economy. My house, which is to say *our house* (Barbara was with me), was about ten minutes from the base. One weekend, while sweeping out the garage, Barbara and I encountered a stray cat that was either hungry, in need of companionship, or both.

Feral cats are common and plentiful throughout Bahrain, surviving on whatever food scraps they can find within the supermarket dumpsters and residential trash cans. Unlike domestic housecats, which are groomed and self-confident, Bahrain's feral cats are dirty and skittish. Occasionally, however, especially around the Navy base and expat housing communities, where sympathetic, animal-loving Westerners reside, feral cats tend to be less apprehensive. Regardless of people's feelings toward cats—and, let's be honest, dog lovers tend to favor canines over felines—most people would agree that cats are intelligent creatures. Moreover, they're adept at pulling on people's heartstrings by purring, meowing, or rubbing against a pant leg for attention.

Habibiti entered our garage slowly, but with a sense of familiarity. She was white with orange accents, and her hazel eyes were shaped liked almonds. Unlike most of Bahrain's feral cats, who seemed suspicious of strangers, the cat that entered our garage did so with a sense of grace. Her tail stood erect like a periscope scanning the horizon. My first reaction was one of uncertainty, but not because I was a dog lover. I was concerned for how Barbara would respond; she loves all animals but is especially fond of cats.

"Poverina," Barbara sighed, squatting to the cat's eye level. "Guarda comé sei magra!" (*Poor little thing, look how skinny you are!*)

"Whatever you do, don't feed it," I cautioned. "We don't need a cat moving in with us."

"Ciao, Habibiti," Barbara cooed, ignoring me. It was love at first sight.

As if prompted by Barbara's audible cues, the cat started purring and doing figure eights; her tail caressed Barbara's arm as she spun in place. I was less concerned with the budding romance than I was by the impact of a stray cat warming up to my sympathetic, animal-loving wife. I could see where this was headed: making friends in the garage would lead to feeding the cat and allowing it to come inside the house, whereby Barbara would have it sleeping on a blanket in our bedroom. Feeling right at home, the cat would start scratching the furniture and leaving cat hair everywhere. In due course, Barbara would expect me to clean out the cat box. Thinking about all the impending consequences was making me agitated.

"Don't pet it," I warned. "You don't know what kind of disease it might have."

"No, no," Barbara countered. "This cat isn't wild, she's been abandoned. Look how clean she is—and friendly, see?"

Barbara was now petting the cat's head while the purring and caressing intensified. I had lost the battle before it even started.

"Whatever," I replied in exasperation, exiting the garage. "Just don't let it in the house, okay?"

Barbara didn't respond. She was mesmerized by her new companion. This was a bad sign, indeed.

Within seconds of laying eyes upon her little friend, Barbara had ascertained its gender as female, determined that the cat's fate had been placed in her hands, and gave it a name: Habibiti. Not to be disrespectful, Barbara ignored my direction and went right to work on providing her new friend something to eat. After fetching a can of tuna fish from the kitchen cupboard, she prepared lunch for the cat in a small dish along with a bowl of water. The Navy had trained me to defend myself in combat but offered nothing in terms of dealing with a wife, who along with a cat, had the ability to outmaneuver me within a matter of minutes.

"Just don't feed her in the house, okay?" I couldn't believe how fast I'd been outflanked.

Before the sun had set, Barbara had gone to the store and bought some cat food. I tried to pretend I wasn't interested, but I couldn't help being impressed by the bond they had established so quickly. The cat seemed interested not only in getting fed, but earning some companionship. Several days later, I decided to break the ice.

"How's your cat doing?"

"Habibiti?" Barbara asked.

The surprise in her voice revealed a moment of weakness. By nature, Italians tend to be competitive, but women from Tuscany can be as hard as Carrara marble. The last thing Barbara would want me to think was that my approval might benefit the objective she was striving to achieve—which was keeping this stray cat as a pet. Curbing her excitement, Barbara shifted gears and continued with a rather poor attempt at trying to appear aloof.

"The cat is fine," she replied.

Barbara's bland response didn't fool me. Sensing how important this had become, I decided to soften my approach.

"She looks healthy. I think she likes it here." *I'm such a pushover. Why am I always the first one to offer the olive branch?*

"She comes to see me every day," Barbara said with a satisfied grin. Her hands were now on her hips as she looked down at her prize, feeling proud of herself. Habibiti was sitting erect, looking up at her savior. This cat had hit the jackpot.

Not wishing to lose all my leverage, I downshifted and applied just a hint of sarcasm: "Ya think? I'd stop by, too, if someone put food out for me every day—just like you're doing for old—*what's her name?*—your little friend, here." Now my hands were on my hips. I looked down at the cat. Habibiti wasn't a bit self-conscious. She sat confidently below us, looking aloof, swishing the floor with her tail.

"Habibiti," Barbara quipped. "Her name is Habibiti." Barbara stated her name as if the two of them had been acquainted for years. They were old pals. They played cribbage every Tuesday night with the girls. The fact that I was the one providing a roof over their heads didn't seem to matter. I had already become the odd man out; three was a crowd.

"The name 'Habibiti' means sweetheart—in Arabic," Barbara added with an air of sophistication.

"Okay, Habibiti," I said. "Stay out of the house."

I couldn't resist having the last word. Having been effectively removed from the equation (already), my pride was the only thing I had left to try and salvage. As I walked away, I looked over my shoulder to see Barbara squatting and grabbing her cat around her waist, gently lifting her off the floor, bouncing her paws up and down. Barbara was caressing her pet while introducing it to the language it would soon become familiar with: Italian.

"Woo-wo-wo! Stai fuori, te! Come sei una bella gattina! Come sei una bella gattina!" (*Baby talk. Stay outside, you! What a pretty little cat you are! What a pretty little cat you are!*)

Looking back, I can see now that I wasn't aware of how significant Habibiti had become to Barbara, and because of this, events that were about to occur would throw our world into chaos.

About three weeks later, there was a thunderstorm in the middle of the night, a highly unusual phenomenon for Bahrain; the desert island receives less than three inches of rainfall per year. The sound of thunder and rain hitting the skylight in the middle of the house woke me up. Barbara was sacked out, buried beneath the covers.

"Would you listen to that?" I said out loud, assuming that Barbara had awoken, too. "Do you think the cat's okay?"

Barbara was awake, but barely. Murmuring beneath the covers, she offered her response to my late-night concern: "She's a cat. I'm sure she's fine."

What happened next defies logic: I went downstairs to check on Habibiti.

"Where are you going?" Barbara asked, poking her head up from beneath the sheets. For a second, she cast an image of *Kilroy*: the top of her head was exposed above the sheets, hands poised on each side of her face, eyes bugged out.

I wasn't prepared to explain myself, so I didn't respond. I just kept making my way down the stairs. Through the sliding glass door, I could see Habibiti sleeping on one of the chairs beneath the patio table. The patio was covered, so Habibiti was dry and appeared comfortable. The wind was blowing hard, and the water in the pool was being pelted by heavy raindrops. I opened the sliding glass door, cradled the cat in my arms, and headed back upstairs. Habibiti didn't struggle. In fact, she seemed content, purring like a little motorboat. The thought occurred to me that she'd been in the house before—despite my instructions to Barbara to leave her outside. Breaking my own rules, I had invited the cat inside, carried her upstairs (which heretofore was well out of bounds), and placed her on the foot of the bed.

"You can sleep here tonight, Habi," I whispered, petting her on the head. Habibiti just yawned, exposing all those sharp teeth. Her breath smelled like dead fish. I may have detected some mouse in there as well.

As I climbed back into bed, I could see that Barbara had been watching me, leaning back on her elbows with a confused look on her face.

"What are you doing?" she asked.

"Shh!" I whispered, throwing my head back on the pillow and pull-ing up the blankets slowly, so as not to disturb the cat who was now wide awake, watching the two of us. Suddenly it occurred to me: *Why was Barbara questioning me over considerations being extended to* her *cat?*

I attempted to explain what had started with good intentions but turned into a bad idea. "She can sleep here tonight," I said. "There's a huge storm outside. The cat might get scared, run out into the street, and get hit by a car." Employing the worst-case scenario always seemed to work, so I went with it.

"Why did you put her on our bed?" Barbara blurted out.

The volume of Barbara's voice seemed to compete with the hard rain that was pelting the skylight. Barb was awake now, that much was for sure.

One of the odd things I discovered about my lovely bride was that she appeared oblivious to the protocols that most people honor be-tween midnight and 7:00 a.m. The wee hours of the morning generally call for muted tones, even whispers. Whenever Barbara is awakened suddenly, however, she expresses herself at decibel levels that are generally reserved for hailing cabs.

Rising from the bed in frustration, Barbara sprang into action. "You don't know what kind of parasites she might have."

"Parasites?" I replied, squinting from the assault upon my ears.

Barbara disappeared into the hallway, flip-flops slapping angrily on the marble floor, and returned within moments with a blanket. Moving deliberately, she lay the folded blanket on a chair in our bed-room, removed the cat from the foot of our bed, and placed it on the blanket. The look on Habibiti's face seemed to say, *Excuse me guys but I prefer the bed, thank you.*

As if she were racing against the clock, Barbara hustled back into bed, threw her head on the pillow, and pulled the covers over her head. A minute later, Habibiti climbed out of the chair and was back on the foot of the bed. Trying to remain patient, Barbara relocated the cat from the bed to the chair three times.

Realizing I was the one who had opened Pandora's box, I remained quiet while the drama between the bed and chair played out. After the third go-round, Barbara gave up, put the blanket on the foot of the bed, and let the cat have her preferred resting place. Needless to say, Habibiti fell asleep, and from that point forward that was where she slept, every night.

Several months later, security concerns resulting from increased terrorist threats throughout Bahrain prompted the base commander to repatriate all the US military dependents back to the US. It was huge ordeal, as military families living with their sponsors were forced to separate. Like everyone else who was impacted by the commander's directive, Barbara and I had to make some adjustments, too. On the eve of her departure, Barbara left explicit instructions on how to take care of her cat. I assured her I'd do everything I could within the parameters I had to work with (cats have minds of their own) while Barbara left for home, heartbroken and frustrated.

Every night, when I returned from work, Habibiti was waiting on the patio. During the day, she had gone out and done her cat thing: killing mice, patrolling the neighborhood, and sleeping on our patio. After dinner, she slept on the couch while I watched TV, and then followed me upstairs to bed. Considering she spent the bulk of her time outdoors, Habibiti kept herself clean and well groomed. Having been born on the streets of Bahrain, however, she wasn't exactly friendly— at least not like a domestic cat. Habibiti was independent; she didn't like being handled or even petted. Having a spot on the couch and the foot of the bed didn't seem to influence her feelings for me in the least.

Several months later, my tour of duty was complete, and it was time to go home. During a telephone conversation with Barbara, she asked the million-dollar question: "What about Habibiti?"

"What about her?" I replied.

"You're bringing her home with you, aren't you?"

I hesitated before relaying the bad news. "No, dear, I'm not bringing the stray cat that was born on the streets of Bahrain back with me to America. She was here when we arrived, and this is where she'll remain. She'll be fine."

I hated to make the hard call, but I had to. Several months prior to being released from active duty, I had made arrangements for a job interview in Europe. With my résumé having been vetted, I was informed that the job was mine, but a formal interview was still required before the contract could be signed. The process of demobilizing from the Navy and relocating overseas required multiple challenges I wasn't willing to negotiate with a cat in tow. In an effort to justify my desire to move forward, with the fewest distractions possible, I convinced myself that the cat would be fine, even if she were left behind. I know that none of this sounds very sympathetic. Some might even say that my indifference toward Habibiti was cruel. And yes, Barbara protested, though not vehemently; she understood what I was trying to accomplish for our future but hoped to find a middle-ground solution. Regretfully, there wasn't one. Habibiti would be left behind.

"You can't abandon a cat," Barbara pleaded. "It's bad luck."

Having to take such a hard stand against Barbara's wishes was hard enough. Listening to more persistent and inflated arguments, however, was starting to test my patience.

"What are you talking about?" I asked sternly. "I don't believe in any kind of luck, Barb—good or bad—and I'm not about to begin by thinking a cat has any influence over our destiny."

"You'll see," she replied, as if she knew something I didn't.

Italians tend to be superstitious. I don't why, but they are. Barbara told me that if you drop a bottle of olive oil and it spills all over the floor you'll have five years of bad luck. Cheating the Italian government by not claiming income is overwhelmingly accepted in Italy, but abandoning a cat will get you five to ten years at Castel St. Angelo in Rome.

"I'll make you a deal," I said into the phone, glad I wasn't looking her in the eye—because the proposal I was about to make was as about as far-fetched a plan that I could come up with—"If the job in Europe pans out, I'll buy you a plane ticket and you can fly back to Bahrain, find your cat, and take her home with you."

I was certain this was an offer I would never have to honor. The silence on the other end of the line indicated that Barbara had realized the futility of continuing the discussion. Bringing the cat home to the US and transporting it with us while we endeavored to restart our lives, would be a burden. Habibiti had in fact been surviving on the streets of Mahooz, and without us she would probably endure.

How well Barbara would cope with the loss was another matter entirely. She had grown very fond of Habibiti and had her heart set on keeping her. Reluctantly, Barbara set her feelings aside, took one for the team, and suffered in silence. Before leaving, I bought several large sacks of cat food and made arrangements with one of the live-in housekeepers across the street to feed and look after the cat. In hopes that the housekeeper would look after the cat, I paid him the equivalent of one month's salary. As I departed from Bahrain, I felt that I done more than my fair share.

What occurred over the next few months was bizarre. I'm talking *Twilight Zone* weird. I'm not superstitious, I don't believe in luck (good or bad), but I will say this: what followed was one of the longest, sustained periods of calamity I've ever had to endure. Everything that could go wrong did go wrong. Barbara blamed it on me, of course. I was the one who had set into motion the dark spell that had been cast upon us.

For all you cat lovers who have been siding with Barbara thus far, here is a list of the catastrophes that ensued after leaving Habibiti behind. If you're a dog person (like me), then you'll no doubt dismiss the following as hyperbole.

After returning to California, I reunited with Barbara to discover that she had been experiencing a great deal of pain in her jaw. I was convinced that it was stress-induced, but when the pain wouldn't subside I took her to the emergency room, where we sat for over six hours, waiting to be seen by a doctor.

"You'd better be dying or something," I warned. "This is taking forever!"

The doctor's assessment concurred with mine: Barbara was suffering from stress; she was clenching her teeth in her sleep. After revealing to the doctor what was causing her stress (Barbara confessed to being worried about a cat that I had "abandoned" in Bahrain), the doctor just stared at us above his reading glasses. I was tempted to ask him to prescribe me with a sedative.

Our trip from California to Europe encompassed flying Space-A aboard MILAIR flights, whereby we would hopscotch across America, catch a flight over the Atlantic, and make our way to our home in Tuscany. Unbeknownst to us at the time was the fact that we were about to embark upon a marathon journey, halfway around the world, and be tested to the limits of our stamina and patience.

The first leg of our journey took off from Travis AFB (northeast of San Francisco) where we caught a KC-135 to Andrews AFB in Washington, DC. Disembarking the aircraft onto a snow-covered tarmac was only the beginning of our problems. We arrived late in the evening, and were unaware that taxis were prohibited from entering the base after 4:00 p.m. The post-9/11 regulation was implemented due to the fact that Andrews AFB is the home of Air Force One, the US president's personal airplane. Without ground transportation, we were forced to walk from the passenger terminal to the main gate, pushing two luggage carts carrying a total of seven suitcases. The walking distance from the terminal to the main gate took us nearly an hour to negotiate. Several airmen drove past us in their pickup trucks. No one seemed to notice our predicament, let alone offer us a lift. As a Navy man, my pride wouldn't consider asking anyone in the Air Force for assistance, so we walked, and we walked, and we nearly froze. Fortunately, there was a Holiday Inn just outside the main gate, where we took refuge for the night.

After breakfast, the next morning, Barbara and I returned to our room to discover that the keycard wouldn't open the door. As it turned out, the problem wasn't the keycard but the locking mechanism in the door. After an hour of failing to gain access, we became concerned that we would miss our next flight. Finally, a hotel maintenance man used an electric saw to cut his way into our room, whereby we gathered up our things and were driven to the airport by an embarrassed hotel manager.

Upon arriving in Norfolk, Virginia, we proceeded by taxi to the naval air station hotel for the evening. As we were checking in, I opened my wallet and realized that the hotel manager in DC had failed to give me back my credit card. After a telephone call confirmed that the hotel manager still had my card, I realized that I had left my $1,000 camera in the trunk of the cab.

With the cat's curse in full swing, the MILAIR flights from Norfolk to Europe were delayed for several days due to maintenance. Never to be deterred, Barbara and I rented a car and drove to Dover AFB in Rhode Island, in hopes of catching an overseas flight. What we learned, however, was that while there were flights, none of them were available for civilian passengers; the C-5 transports headed across the pond were carrying ordnance to resupply the war effort. Three weeks earlier, I had flown from Afghanistan to Qatar aboard a C-17, carrying bombs and ammunition, but I wasn't a civilian at the time. I was still in uniform. As such, Uncle Sam considered me expendable. Not only was I allowed on board, I was permitted to unbuckle from my seat and catch a nap between two pallets of Hellfire rockets.

Two days after arriving in Dover, we drove back to Norfolk and caught a hop to Rota, Spain. Upon our arrival, however, we couldn't find any flights headed in the direction of our final destination. *Not a problem. We'll go sightseeing for a few days.* While touring the Spanish countryside, I entered a parking lot at a roadside rest stop. Failing to notice the boulders that had been placed as parking bumpers, I rolled our rental car over the top of a 300-pound rock that nearly ripped out the undercarriage.

From Rota, Spain, we finally caught a hop to NAS Sigonella in Sicily, only to learn that the next available flight to the Italian mainland was in five days. *No worries, we'll take the train and catch the ferry.* To our astonishment, however, a freak 500-year storm had hit the island the night before. A hillside next to the train tracks collapsed, washed out the railway, and put the southern half of Sicily's transportation network out of commission. *Bravissimo!*

Ten days after leaving California, we finally arrived at our home in Tuscany, rested for a few days, and rented a car for the drive up to Luxembourg. The weather in Europe was cold and snowy, but I took my time, hoping to avoid another catastrophe. After completing my job interview, I was walking back to the car, thinking about when I might be able to start my new job. Consumed by my thoughts, I slipped on some ice on the snow-covered parking lot and fractured my wrist.

Three weeks after the interview, I finally received a formal job offer to work as a NATO consultant. Despite being told that my services would be required for six months, I was only offered a position for four weeks.

Determined to succeed, I accepted the assignment in the hope of receiving an offer to extend—which eventually came through; I was asked to stay for another two whole months. *Whoopee!* Had the curse been lifted? Not hardly. While going through my bank statement I discovered that the Italian rental car company we were using had illegally appropriated $2,500 from my credit card. It took a year to get reimbursed for 70 percent of the stolen funds. I digested the balance and swore never to do business with the company again.

Despite the bumpy start, I enjoyed the change of pace that came with living in Europe. I wore a coat and tie, rode the train to work, and collaborated with colleagues from other countries in support of common objectives. I had concerns associated with the brevity of my contract, however, and the short-term solution involved securing a hotel on the Luxembourg-Belgium border.

While I was at work, Barbara tended to the domestic chores, making sure my clothes were clean and pressed for the following day. She spent much of her time reading and mapping out sites for us to see during the weekends. When I returned from work in the evenings an aperitif was waiting. While snacking on chips and sipping the local wine, we talked about the weather and my job, and toasted our future with fingers crossed. Afterward, Barbara put on a dress and I took her out for a nice dinner. It was the least I could do for the woman who had followed me around the world. Despite concerns for our uncertain future, Barbara waited patiently for my return from work each day. She sat in that hotel room alone, watching the rain, feeling glum, and missing her cat.

Barbara has always been a great traveler and she enjoys experiencing new cultures and foreign destinations. She likes to know where she's headed, however, and deep down I knew she was having trouble adapting to the cold climate, not seeing the sun for days at time, and wondering about the fate of her cat, Habibiti. With our rented car parked at the hotel each day, she could have ventured into Luxembourg City, taken in some sights, or done some shopping, but she opted against it. Barbara grew up on the coast of the Mediterranean, she didn't know how to drive in the snow, and she was feeling depressed. The gloomy skies, the cold, damp weather, and Barbara's disposition were merging together like a fog bank rolling into a deep, endless swamp. Barbara is a fighter, but she was losing that battle, and I was concerned.

Barbara thought that her prayers had been answered when I returned from work one evening and announced that I had been offered a position in Kabul to oversee a pair of military construction projects. My new position in Afghanistan meant that Barbara could move as well. She opted to return to Bahrain. Within hours after landing there, we rented a car and began searching the old neighborhood for our cat, Habibiti. She was nowhere to be found. On the following day, we returned and saw her walking next to our former residence.

In the five months we'd been away she'd lost half her body weight. Scratched and bloodied from street fights, Habibiti appeared to have expended at least eight of her nine lives; her sabbatical with Barbara had softened her survival skills.

Barbara and I fed and watered Habibiti twice a day. After the morning feeding, we'd go out and look at rental properties and return in the afternoon. Habibiti seemed to recognize us but was leery and afraid. Re-earning her trust would be Barbara's job; mine was to find a house for Barbara (and her cat) before heading to Afghanistan and starting my new job. Within a couple of days, we located and rented a suitable villa. After helping Barbara get her affairs in order, I departed for my new assignment. A week later, Barbara put Habibiti in the car and brought her to the new house. Habibiti hid under the sofa for a week.

Over the next few months, Habibiti fattened up and reconnected with her human caretaker, the Italian woman she had met in Al Mahooz, the woman who unsuccessfully argued against her abandonment, endured months of misfortune (perhaps as a result thereof), and willed her way to finding her again. This was a love story that deserved a happy ending.

My first eighteen months in Afghanistan were successful. The NATO agency offered me a full-time position and I was directed to return to Luxembourg as a member of the home office's military infrastructure program. I was required to travel back and forth between Luxembourg and Afghanistan several times a year. Fortunately, however, at least for the time being, the day-to-day drudge that I had endured downrange had been set aside.

Relocating Barbara from Bahrain to Luxembourg was less challenging the second time in that she was familiar with the terrain and our future had been secured by a good job and comfortable salary. Not wishing to tempt fate (twice), I agreed to bring Habibiti with us. Before leaving Bahrain, Barbara brought her cat to the vet to have her spayed and vaccinated. The vet discovered some infected molars that had to be pulled and explained that Habibiti had been quietly suffering.

"She never appeared to be in any pain," Barbara said to the vet.

"Felines instinctively conceal pain as a defense mechanism against potential predators," the vet explained.

Barbara wasn't exactly keen on moving back to Luxembourg, but being a supportive wife, she rolled with the changes and was consoled by the fact that her cat would accompany her. As for the cat, Habibiti's life changed as well. The climate and living conditions in Luxembourg were a far cry from the life she had lived in the perpetually warm climate of Arabia. In Luxembourg, the weather was cold, it rained constantly, and Habibiti wasn't permitted to venture outside the house and explore the neighborhood; Barbara kept her indoors for fear that she'd be hit by a car on the busy street in front of our house.

Habibiti didn't mind. She moved freely about the house and appeared content with her new surroundings.

Sadly, within six months of relocating to Luxembourg, Habibiti developed inoperable cancer and had to be euthanized. Barbara was devastated, and I felt helpless, unable to offer solace. I buried our Habibiti in the garden and planted some flowers on her grave. Barbara keeps a picture of her cat, and we still share stories about how she touched our lives.

Several other cats have crossed paths with us since Habibiti passed away, and with every new encounter I've come to understand and appreciate the feline species even more. Ironically, and however unfortunate Habibiti's passing may have been, reconnecting with her in Bahrain proved not only to put an end to the curse of the cat, good fortune seemed to smile upon us like rays of sunshine beaming from above.

CHAPTER EIGHT

War Is Hell

"War is hell, but it certainly makes for some good financial opportunities."

I can't count the number of times I used to say that, but I did, especially on payday.

As contractors, we benefited from the flow of cash associated with the business of war, and the local inhabitants of Afghanistan benefited as well. Afghan merchants and entrepreneurs learned quickly that coalition forces and their contractors had a huge appetite for provisions. Food, furnishings, fuel, vehicles, construction equipment, and labor provided the lifeblood that sustained the war. Ironically, the war was being prosecuted upon the very people that the Afghan merchants interacted with. How did the locals justify such treason? They didn't; war is hell, and everyone understood that they had to take what they could while the getting was good.

Self-preservation through commerce with the enemy didn't sit well with the Taliban and the insurgency. Their goal was to cut off their adversary's ability to make war—not sustain it. During a restoration project of a large aircraft hangar at Kandahar Airfield (the KILO hangar, for those readers who served on KAF), a truckload of steel arrived with the codriver lying dead in the front seat. He'd been shot during an ambush while en route to the base. War is hell, but we got our steel and completed the project.

In the spring of 2010, my Turkish employers received a subcontract to repave the runway at Shindand Air Base. Shindand is on the western outskirts of Afghanistan, about eighty kilometers from the Iranian border. To facilitate the construction of the new runway the Turks needed to deploy a thirty-eight-ton, million-dollar concrete paving machine. The Turks owned a total of three concrete pavers. Not all of them were in use so they decided to transport one of the idle machines from a project on BAF to the runway project in Shindand. The challenge would entail moving the paver a distance of over 800 kilometers across the badlands of Afghanistan. The Turks were nervous because of an encounter they'd had while shipping a mobile concrete batch plant to the same jobsite a month earlier. While en route with the batch plant, the transport truck got caught in an ambush and the equipment sustained some damage. If memory serves me, the driver of the truck was also injured.

Apprehensive over the risks associated with a similar movement, my employers were hoping to find an alternative solution. The Turks were in luck, for while on active duty in Bahrain I spent six months working in the Logistics Operation Cell (LOC) at Naval Central Command (forward) in Bahrain. My responsibilities included coordinating air movements throughout Iraq and Afghanistan. I was intimately familiar with the military's policy of providing opportune airlifts to contractors requesting support for their strategically sensitive projects. The process of vetting the airlift request required the submittal of a specific form, which took a week for the USAF's air logistics center at Al Udeid, Qatar, to review and approve/disapprove. Most requests were approved, but it usually took several weeks to procure an available aircraft.

The USAF's C-17 Globemaster is a cargo-carrying beast of an aircraft that can carry a maximum payload of 130,000 pounds, or sixty-five tons. I knew that the thirty-eight-ton track-moving paver could be driven into the belly of the C-17 with room and weight to spare. After discussing our delivery plan to the US prime contractor (who had hired our company to repave the runway) the request was rejected—but not by the Air Force. The runway project's PM, a belligerent bully, had ambushed the idea before it was even submitted to the Air Force for review. Claiming he had spoken to the Air Force and that the airlift wasn't possible, the project PM shot a sharply worded email to my company, demanding we make haste and ship the paver via truck and trailer—immediately. When I received news that the PM had squashed our request —without the benefit of having filled out the appropriate request form, no less—I was suspicious.

Anxious to appease their new customer, the compliant Turks contracted with a commercial freight company who manifested the paver within a 300-vehicle super convoy. The wagon train of diesel rigs stretched from one end of the horizon to the other. Cargo convoys of such immense size were common along Afghanistan's ring route, as were the road agents, hijackers, and assassins lying in wait for an opportunity to pounce. Dispersed among the convoy were armed mercenaries to fend off would-be attackers.

Ninety kilometers into the journey, the midsummer scorching-hot highway claimed its first victim: a tire beneath the trailer carrying the paving machine disintegrated. Armed escorts waited while the tire was changed, but shortly after resuming the journey a second tire failed. Stuck along the highway without another spare, the truck driver made a series of unsuccessful cell phone calls for assistance. Anxious to rejoin the convoy, the armed guards left the wounded rig behind. The driver and codriver opted to stay with the truck in hopes of resolving their issues on the following day.

Shortly after nightfall, the paver truck was ambushed. The driver was killed, but the codriver escaped into the desert. While trying to make off with their prize, the road warriors buried the truck's axles in the sand along the side of the road. Frustrated, they set the tractor ablaze and abandoned their booty. The codriver called for help and the Turks immediately dispatched a rescue squad to retrieve their million-dollar cargo. The rescuers tried unsuccessfully throughout the day to hire another truck to pull the load to safety, but as the sun began to set the effort was put in recess and the rescue crews retreated. When they returned in the morning, the salvage crew arrived at the scene of a smoldering hulk of steel. The assailants had returned during the night to destroy what they couldn't use steal.

Photo by Unknown Afghan who was on scene

In the wake of the attack, we still needed a concrete paver for the project in Shindand. When the Turks came to me for a suggestion on how to ship yet another paver, I responded with frustration: "My answer is the same as the one I gave before: we're going to airlift our paver aboard a C-17—but don't bother asking that PM for permission this time. I'll take care of it."

Weeks later, the backup paver arrived in Shindand after being airlifted aboard a C-17. I don't recall seeing an email from the prime contractor, offering condolences for our million-dollar loss, a letter of thanks for successfully procuring a second paver, or a kind thought for the deceased driver—but that was to be expected; war is hell, and those who contributed to the misery routinely got away with murder.

For US and foreign civilian contractors who supported the war effort, there were risks and rewards. Many Afghan entrepreneurs became millionaires, while others were kidnapped and murdered as traitors.

To mitigate their exposure, construction companies employed creative solutions that enabled them to complete their projects with minimal losses. One solution involved the production of on-site-produced concrete, and the hiring of locals to help run the plants. Some of the concrete batch plants were located inside the wire, thereby affording the workers military protection. Most of the batch plants, however, were located off-base along the perimeter fence, making them vulnerable to attacks—without the aid of the military's defenses.

Transporting concrete from an off-base plant, through the military entry control point (ECP), could also be time-consuming and costly. Failing to place a batch of concrete within a specific period of time (after its been produced) will create a chemical imbalance in the mixture, and entire load will be lost.

An alternative solution to waiting in line at the ECP (and risk losing loads of concrete) was to send the mud over the fence through a trough. The over-the-fence method also proved to be a valuable force protection remedy in that concrete trucks could be rigged to carry

Photo from author's collection.

large quantities of explosives. Keeping the trucks inside the wire was a clever way to reduce the threat of vehicle-born improvised explosive devices (VBIEDs), eliminate the risk of the concrete spoiling, and speed-up production.

The provision of jobs to locals provided revenue for both the Afghan workers and the tribal chiefs they were obliged to tithe. The flow of money also helped to keep the peace, as locals receiving money were less apt to kill their unwelcome guests. Satisfying the indigenous population's irrepressible needs was a science in itself, however, and disputes often arose. In the midst of a disagreement between two neighboring villages (who were providing laborers to one of our off-base concrete plants), a disgruntled local struck one of our security guards over the head with a pipe, killing him. A second guard shot the pipe-wielding Afghan. He died as well. To avoid further conflict, my employers met with the village elder from the deceased Afghan's tribe and agreed to pay a settlement fee of $15,000. The fee guaranteed peace and the continuation of relations that permitted the Turks to retain their low-cost labor force. Considering that the annual per capita income for the average Afghan was just over $500, the $15,000 settlement went a long way.

Over the years, I encountered several instances involving the death of a local citizen, and $15,000 seemed to be the going rate for the life of an Afghan. A year earlier, one of our employees struck and killed a local child with his car. My employers agreed to pay the village elder $15,000. War was hell, but whether it was the life of an Afghan or the bottom line upon which a contractor would agree to risk his or her life, everything seemed to have a price.

Having to cope with the challenges associated with living in a war zone required both patience and a sense of humor. Reminding myself (and others) that "war is hell" was an understatement, but when I caveated that our predicament made for some good financial opportunities it seemed to take the edge off; people chuckled at the irony they'd become a part of. Of course, there were alternatives: if you couldn't stand the heat then you got out of the kitchen. I didn't observe a large number of contractors turning tail and going home during the war; the US economy had stagnated, and the job market in America wasn't offering much to displaced workers and failed small-business owners. US and NATO-funded contracts throughout Afghanistan amounted to billions of dollars in revenue each year, which offered tens of thousands of jobs for contractors and employees of companies that supported the war effort—from all over the world. If you were one of the contractors working downrange, however, there was a catch: you wouldn't be going home that often—and you might get killed. *I don't recall seeing that in the fine print...did I agree to those terms?*

Civilian contractors never actually said it, but there was an implied consent to accept the danger that came with the territory. The terms of the agreement were akin to being voluntary trustees of a psychiatric ward, whereby the patients were free to leave at any time. I suspect that most of us chose to remain in Afghanistan for fear of what we'd encounter beyond the walls of the asylum, and when you think about it, agreeing to take a job where your life literally hung in the balance each day sounds a bit insane. I was equally impressed by the number of people who appeared content by the mediocre and sometimes dangerous conditions we lived in. Over time, I came to appreciate the colorful palette of different people I worked with by putting our collective situations into perspective: I viewed my colleagues as dedicated folks who were doing what they felt was necessary to keep the home fires burning. I admired them for having the courage to face challenges that most people would never embark upon. Some of us seemed a bit fearless at times, and that helped, too.

Having lived and worked in such conditions for years at a time provided me—and the majority of hard-core contractors with whom I associated—the confidence we needed to choose between returning home, or staying downrange for the duration of however long good fortune (or survival) would allow. We understood the tradeoffs and were not uncomfortable with the risks. Enduring the highs, the lows, and even the doldrums of being in combat seemed to nurture an attitude that was equivalent to acquiring an armor coating. I was privileged to work among some of the finest and toughest people on Earth. Your typical seasoned contractor was like a rhinoceros: a peaceful yet powerful creature that spends most of its time minding its own business. Whenever provoked, however, a rhino will wreak havoc. Pissing off a forward-deployed contractor who was living in a stinky, thirty-year-old twelve-man tent or a plywood-constructed B-Hut could lead to similar results.

Living under conditions that cultivated prickly and ambivalent attitudes had a way of desensitizing people. I remember lying in bed reading a book one evening when the sound of an incoming rocket came whistling into the FOB. My well-trained ears determined that the threat wasn't close; it was heading away from me toward the other side of the base. As the rocket impacted, it exploded with a low reverberating rumble. The explosion wasn't loud, but I could tell it was powerful. Upon hearing the explosion, I remember commenting to myself sarcastically, "Wow, sucks being them." The following morning, over breakfast, I learned that two people had perished and several others had been wounded.

Had the attack occurred during the first few months of my career in Afghanistan, I might have felt differently; I might have felt fear, sorrow for the victims, remorse over my insensitive comment, and perhaps even trepidation over my own fate. On that day, however, several years after arriving in Afghanistan, having survived numerous rocket attacks and a list of terrible events, I didn't feel much of anything at all—which is sad, really, but that's what war does to people; it dulls their senses.

It wouldn't be unfair to say that as a group, civilian contractors developed a habit of nurturing what became a set of unbalanced values. I had many colleagues and friends whose careers in war zone contracting started with a clear path they intended to follow, but over time trajectories tended to veer off course. After being beaten down by years of recession, the opportunity for financial recovery and a chance at prosperity, was hard to resist. During the height of the war, therefore—which lasted over a decade—the possibilities for acquiring the good life and putting away some money for the future were palpable.

I had a friend I'll refer to as Jimmy, a dedicated colleague who had a wife and a couple of kids back in the States. Prior to the collapse of the US economy, Jimmy's construction business was booming. He was a good provider, and his family lived in a nice home. Jimmy was also a model citizen within his community. After years of trying (unsuccessfully) to recover from the catastrophic collapse of his business, Jimmy was broke, financially and spiritually. A once-confident, successful, and proud man, Jimmy was running from creditors and feeling like a failure. By opting for hazardous duty, Jimmy was hoping for a chance at redemption. Given the magnitude of debt he had incurred, however, he had his work cut out for him.

It took several years, but eventually Jimmy caught up on most of his liabilities and was starting to see the light at the end of the tunnel. Instead of reentering the atmosphere of the real world, however, Jimmy chose to remain in orbit. To his credit, Jimmy had adapted well to challenges of working downrange. He had his own sleeping container (wet) and earned himself an elevated position as a project manager overseeing several construction projects valued at over $50 million. In essence, Jimmy had become an important man again, and it felt good.

Back home, the wife and kids, who struggled during the initial months while Jimmy was away, had adjusted quite well in spite of his absence. How well? Enough to have grown used to the fact that Jimmy rarely came home anymore. Once the money starting flowing, everyone seemed to forget who had turned on the tap. The kids were wearing the best tennis shoes, taking karate lessons after private school, and being entertained by the latest video games. Jimmy's wife was able to quit her job and become a stay-at-home mom—for the first time in their marriage—and she spent much of her time decorating their new house. Weekly trips to the nail salon and the gym (where her younger and quite handsome personal trainer kept her in proper form) provided her with all the distractions she needed while daddy was away.

Meanwhile, back in "the Stan," Jimmy stayed busy, juggling a long list of tasks each day. Much to his delight, his financial recovery plan had taken seed. After three years working downrange, his back taxes had been satisfied. Most of the debt his failed business had incurred was being paid off, and his family, despite seeing them only a few times each year, appeared healthy and in good spirits. "It's all good," Jimmy told me. "All I have to do is stay in the game for a few more years and I'll return home—for good."

Unfortunately, Jimmy had become so consumed by his work that he failed to notice the warning signs that had been blinking on the horizon. When he received word from his wife that she wanted a divorce, Jimmy was devastated. *The road to hell is paved with good intentions.*

I sympathized with Jimmy. I witnessed similar conditions in other colleagues and had some baggage of my own. I, too, had lost contact with my children. My circumstances differed from what Jimmy experienced, but the catalysts were identical; the war and everything that came with it created unique obstacles that were unfamiliar and difficult for most people to recognize, let alone overcome.

I missed my kids, but like Jimmy's children, mine had adjusted to my absence. My ex-wife remarried a successful yet haughty businessman who was gregarious, and generous. I didn't care for the man, but by all appearances he was well received by my kids—so much so, perhaps, that my children seemed uninterested in whatever their real father was doing. *Go figure.* Teenagers can be terribly selfish, so I tried not to feel bad when the birthday and Christmas presents I sent were rarely acknowledged. A Father's Day card, birthday card, or Christmas card from my kids would have been a nice gesture, but after the first couple of disappointments I stopped waiting for the surprises that never came.

The success I earned as a war zone contractor was overshadowed by years of sadness and uncertainty over the loss of contact with my three children. Feeling defeated, guilty for my role as a failed parent, and deserving of my fate, I withdrew. I stopped calling, emailing, and sending unacknowledged gifts. Sadder still was the fact that no one seemed to notice. I suspect that by giving them space I had made them think I was okay with the status quo. In reality, I was heartbroken. Among all the lessons I learned in Afghanistan, none were as profound as the fact that while *absence may make the heart grow fonder*, it's not a guarantee.

Winning streaks have a way of clouding people's perceptions of reality. The list of celebrities who have met with untimely and premature death is a testament to people's inability to manage all the changes that come with good fortune. The windfall experienced by average folks earning lofty salaries in Afghanistan was no different, but the symptoms of people drowning in their own success were not always apparent. Once the initial shock wore off, of living in an impoverished country, where death and destruction were not uncommon, even the most timid people found ways to adapt. The length of time people served in combat was a testament to the human condition, in terms of durability and forgetfulness. Durability (for example) could be measured in terms of how people acquired the ability to endure the repetition of nightly rocket attacks. I was never completely immune to the sound of an explosion, but appearances could be deceiving; I arrived at the point where I could hear an incoming round explode and appear unmoved. *Been there, done that.*

I wasn't always such a cool operator. Like most people, I get startled by unexpected noises, especially very loud ones.

I recall my first rocket attack in vivid detail. I was at Kandahar Airfield, and I had just fallen asleep. The sound of the rocket spinning toward the earth, followed by a thunderous explosion, was something I had not experienced, and which I'll never forget. I remember waking up feeling confused and scared. Moments later, I heard an announcement crackling over the public address system, directing everyone on the military base to don their protective body armor and proceed to the nearest bomb shelter. Over the next four hours, I got in and out of bed three times. After several weeks of interrupted sleep and constant fatigue, I found the sirens to be an annoyance. As the rockets always exploded ahead of the alarms, I came to realize the futility of trying to avoid a catastrophic event I couldn't control. In other words, if a rocket were to come crashing through my sleeping container I'd probably be killed. Moments later, the siren would sound. *Thanks for the warning!*

With that in mind, I chose to stay in bed while the alarms sounded. Did I feel guilty, lying in bed, while the rest of the camp's inhabitants were donning their flak gear, trotting half-asleep to the nearest bomb shelter, and waiting another thirty to ninety minutes for the all-clear sirens to sound? Not in the least. During subsequent attacks, I was often awakened by the sounds of people conversing outside my window from the nearby bomb shelter. Upon hearing this, I would giggle and go back to sleep. Staying in bed in the middle of a rocket attack was my personal act of defiance. I was winning the War on Terror all by my lonesome. Over time, I developed the ability to sleep through the alarms, which from my point of view was an advantage; I woke up fresh as a daisy, ready to take on a new day.

The forgetfulness factor followed the durability of the human spirit. Taking risks in the war zone and feeling comfortable within an environment where people routinely came face-to-face with disaster was no different from driving a car. Student drivers are nervous the first few times they get behind the wheel, but within a relatively short period of time they forget their fears and head out onto the open road—texting their friends.

It wouldn't be fair to suggest that most drivers feel comfortable texting while driving, but you get the drift. Experience oftentimes leads to overconfidence and complacency, and whenever that occurs, trouble tends to follow.

I recall one particular morning after our FOB was attacked by enemy rockets, and I remember it well because it was Christmas day. A colleague of mine named Blu, a hardcore builder from Utah, had everyone at the breakfast table laughing when he said, "Did you guys hear that rocket that came in last night right after midnight, the one that exploded near our LSA? Man, that was good one!" Blu's eyes were as big as saucers, and he had a smile that stretched from ear to ear. He appeared content knowing that he had skirted disaster and robbed the Grim Reaper out of a commission. Blu's naïveté was entertaining to us old-timers, those of us who'd been downrange for several years. We would smile whenever a rookie got a charge out of something we'd experienced too often. On the surface, our reactions to these events appeared ambivalent; we'd seen it all before so it wasn't a big deal.

Our familiarity with rocket attacks and other events related to living in the combat environment wasn't something to be proud of, however. It was a burden that quietly tallied its woeful sum in the back of our minds, growing with every passing month.

The rookies always had questions about what to do during an attack, or where to go, so the old-timers helped by providing them with a rundown of what to expect. Invariably, the actual events were never quite the same as they were described, they were worse. Having been briefed by your colleagues added a measure of assurance that these events (however unpredictable or frightening) were for the most part survivable, because the risk of getting injured or killed wasn't actually that high. The enemy, who were shooting at us with poorly constructed rockets that failed to detonate much of the time, couldn't hit the broad side of a barn. Most of the rockets failed to reach their designated targets, but on occasion, some would find pay dirt and actually destroy something or cause human casualties.

'Twas the night before Christmas when Blu experienced his first rocket attack. In recognition of the holiday, our Taliban neighbors living on the other side of the wire had traded their finest sheep for some rockets with warheads that actually exploded on impact. I'd already been downrange for over six years so getting bombarded in the middle of the night was something I'd experienced before. Since it was Christmas, I expected the enemy to try and ruin our holiday, and they nearly succeeded.

It was twenty minutes after midnight, Christmas morning, and I had only been asleep for fifteen minutes when the rocket came spiraling in. The warhead detonated less than one hundred meters from our LSA, but even at that distance no one was safe. The blast zone from a 105 mm rocket reaches out for several hundred meters. The detonation produced concussive forces that were so powerful they shook me from my slumber in a way I hadn't experienced in years. I heard the incoming rocket in my sleep, but I wasn't certain I wasn't dreaming until the concussion nearly threw me out of bed. The blast was so powerful, it could only mean one thing: the rocket had impacted very close to our camp. I awoke startled and angry; I would spend another Christmas in a container, getting shot at. *Happy holidays.*

When I came to my senses, I got on my cell phone to call Blu. When he didn't pick up, I suspected he'd left his room to go and check on his friend Dave. Dave was a new hire who had arrived in Afghanistan less than twelve hours earlier. As a newbie, he had no idea that the threats we dealt with were this close. *Welcome aboard, Dave.*

Throwing on my T-shirt and fleece jacket, I went outside to hunt for Blu. As soon as I opened the door I could smell powder from the blast. Dust from the explosion was still raining down on our camp, indicating just how close the rocket had come. When I found Blu walking around outside, I confronted him.

"Blu...what the hell are you doing out here?"

"I wanted to see where that rocket exploded. Man, that was a good one!"

"Yeah, that was a good one," I replied, exasperated yet relieved to see that he was okay.

Everyone else on base was probably throwing on their body armor and running for the bomb shelters. Meanwhile, Blu and I were standing out there in the cold, wearing nothing but jackets over our bare chests, skivvies, and flip-flops.

The hour was late, and we were starting to shiver. Blu said, "Good night," and went to go and check on Dave—who was either too scared to move or smart enough to remain in his container during the attack. When I finally made it back to bed, I had trouble falling asleep. I popped in a DVD and watched it until I couldn't keep my eyes open anymore. I'm not one to feel sorry for myself, but between the stress of being awakened by such a close call and the notion that I should have been home for the holidays, I was feeling glum. As I drifted off to sleep, it occurred to me that war was in fact hell, and on the night before Christmas our enemy was winning.

Indeed, war was hell, and the frustration that came with it was companion to those who made our living on the battlefield. Ironically, most of us felt confident we could defeat the enemy; our troops had both the will and the latest warfighting technology to exert great pain and achieve victory. The overwhelming consensus, however, was that the political strategy was flawed. The idea of earning the hearts and minds among a population who didn't give a lick about us seemed stupid. One day, we'd bomb a village harboring insurgents, and the next we'd be handing out blankets to locals who had been aiding and abetting the enemy.

Bagram Airfield was encircled by local villages containing people who worked with us on the base during the day, and had a side job trying to kill us during the night. Periodically, rocket and mortar attacks were launched from these villages, but oddly enough, very little seemed to be done about it. When a mortar exploded in the bedroom of a sleeping fireman, killing him in his sleep, my buddies and I were pissed; we couldn't understand why harsh measures weren't imposed on every civilian village that could have been responsible. After hearing about the attack from a neighboring village, Blu became irritated and proposed a solution: "They should torch every one of those villages. That'll stop them from shooting at us."

"Sounds like a plan," said Blu's buddy Dave. "Here, use my lighter."

All kidding aside, no one wanted to see innocent people get killed, but to our dismay, we couldn't tell the good ones from the bad. We remembered the words of President George W. Bush, who said, "Every nation in every region, now has a decision to make. Either you are with us, or you are with the terrorists."

I watched the President on TV when he gave that speech, and I believe he meant what he said. After several years of fighting in Afghanistan, however, the tone of the war changed. Many of the politicians (who originally supported the war) seemed unwilling to let the military do what they were trained to do: wreak havoc and persuade the enemy to give in.

During a USO show at Kandahar Airfield, several comedians were brought in from the US to provide entertainment. The off-color jokes about sex and recreational drug use didn't get many laughs; no one in the audience was inclined to link themselves as possible violators of the military's painfully persistent anti-sexual harassment campaign or its zero-tolerance for drug use policy. During the performance, several rockets came screaming into the FOB and exploded somewhere off in the distance. The comedian onstage froze in fear. A uniformed soldier pulled the petrified man from the stage while his colleagues were hustled into the bomb shelters. Meanwhile, the audience shuffled toward the bunkers as directed by the Giant Voice, which could be heard echoing throughout the FOB. We'd seen it all before, so no one was alarmed by the excitement of a rocket two that hadn't even come close.

After the all-clear sirens had sounded, the performance resumed and the comedian returned. Excited and sounding as if he was out of breath, the comedian ranted for minutes over how scared he'd felt during the attack. His ad-libbed skit included a humorous description, rife with expletives, describing the fear he had experienced both onstage and while holed up in the bomb shelter. People chuckled at the comic's exaggerated description, and for the first time that evening, the audience was starting to connect with the entertainment. Suddenly, from the middle of the crowd, someone shouted at the stage, "Welcome to my world, asshole!" The pithy comment generated a roar of approval from the audience, and the comedian burst into laughter. Throughout the rest of the show, the crowd loosened up. We felt empathy for the comedians who'd earned our acceptance as a result of their baptism by fire.

The world I lived in during my service as a contractor hardened my mind and my soul. Some of the things my contractor buddies and I saw and experienced would astonish most people, but we accepted them as par for the course. Achieving such hardness meant the difference between success and failure, stability and uncertainty.

I didn't realize that my experience in the Land of Not Quite Right would make it harder to return to the real world, where there were no conflicts of such magnitude. Oddly enough, the absence of conflict would become a problem in itself. I had become so accustomed to dealing with extraordinary circumstances that life itself, even in its most peaceful context, seemed out of sorts.

CHAPTER NINE

Whiskey, Tango, Foxtrot

During the course of events that took place each day, there were those that caught some of us off guard. Seeing the local butcher's cuts of meat covered with flies and herds of goats feeding on putrefying mounds of garbage paled in comparison to the shocking image of Bibi Aisha on the August 9, 2010 cover of *Time* magazine. Bibi Aisha's father bequeathed his twelve-year-old daughter to marry a Taliban warrior. After enduring years of domestic brutality, Aisha escaped. Several years later, she was found and returned to her husband. For dishonoring her spouse's family, Aisha's husband, his father, and two other family members overpowered Aisha, severed her nose and ears with a knife, and left her for dead.

Within the vast lexicon of the verbiage used in the war zone, there were three words in particular that contractors and warfighters used to describe such befuddling and bizarre acts of barbarism, and those three words were: *whiskey tango foxtrot.*

We didn't actually say those words, per se; *whiskey tango foxtrot* represents the first letter of the US military's phonetic alphabet for each of the corresponding words of that particular phase. Example: the spelling of the word *Army* would by expressed using each letter from the phonetic alphabet as follows: Alfa, Romeo, Mike, and Yankee. Whenever you hear someone say the words *whiskey tango foxtrot* or pronounce the letters *WTF*, therefore, you can be assured that they mean something quite different. It also bears mentioning that the use of this phrase has a special meaning, at least to those of us who were prone to saying it. To certain elements of society, whose numbers I dare say are sadly declining, Whiskey, Tango, Foxtrot, spoken in its unedited form, is a vile expression, rude and indicative of vocabulary used by prison inmates, carneys, and dare I say, my fellow contractors and me.

WTF is summary statement, an exclamation point, a stinger. It means that you've witnessed something beyond belief. You're thoroughly frustrated, taken completely off guard. Flabbergasted beyond words. Some classic examples of when people used the WTF expression include the following:

- The attack on the New York World Trade Center towers. *What the f**k...?*
- The US government's negligent response to (and cover-up of) the attacks on the US embassy and CIA compound at Benghazi: *What the f**k!*
- Directing US contractors (American citizens) to queue in the same lines with local Afghans while awaiting entry into a US military base. *"Hey corporal, what's wrong with this picture? I have security clearance. I mean, what the f**k, dude!?"*

The following are a few anecdotes of when I, along with some of my colleagues, felt compelled to utter what I referred to as three magic words: *Whiskey, Tango, Foxtrot.*

As I drove through the final gate, leaving the base, I set my mind in motion for another solo trek across the desert. It was a lovely afternoon for a Sunday drive, but my focus wouldn't be on the scenery. For the next sixty to ninety minutes, my head would be on a swivel, looking for signs of trouble.

Today's excursion took me from Bagram Airfield (BAF) to Kabul via Route Bottle. The US military gave code names to the roads they used and patrolled. Route Bottle was one of two main highways between Kabul and Bagram. Before 2011, Route Bottle was in pretty bad shape. Afghanistan doesn't have a transportation agency looking after its small network of highways, so the roads were often washed out by floods, rutted with deep potholes, and otherwise neglected. One of the worst sections of highway was an eight-mile stretch from the top of the mountain pass that dropped down into Parwan Valley. Driving the roads of Afghanistan came with risks, and "the Bottle" was a well-known thoroughfare for ambushes and IED attacks. The charred remains of fuel trucks and an assortment of bullet-riddled vehicles routinely lined the highway.

I traveled the roads of Afghanistan, with and without security forces, on many occasions. Often, I made the trip alone, but to many people's astonishment I rarely felt concerned for my safety. Between the military training I'd received in the Navy, a keen sense of situational awareness, and an adventurous *let's see what destiny has in store next* attitude, I was sufficiently equipped to venture out alone.

The highways of Afghanistan consisted of three primary threats: thieves, kidnappers, and assassins. The thieves were your typical highwaymen—road pirates and opportunists who weren't associated with the Taliban, Al-Qaida, or the insurgency—though if pressed to proclaim allegiance, they'd probably side with whoever was asking. Thieves preyed upon convoys, took whatever cargo they could acquire (either peacefully or by forceful means), and sold their merchandise to the highest bidders.

Kidnapping and hostage-taking for ransom was common, but it may surprise people to note that most of the locals who were captured were often released once the ransoms were paid. Americans and other foreign expats were less fortunate. They usually didn't fare as well. Early in my career, I was given a driver who would escort me wherever I needed to go. I never felt comfortable as a passenger, however, so I made a habit of taking the wheel while the driver rode shotgun. My drivers generally found this odd (no one had driven them before), but I didn't care; for all I knew, they might drive me into a trap (and turn me over to the insurgency) or fall asleep at the wheel and drive over a cliff. Eventually, I decided to substitute my driver for weapons and ammo. Traveling with an AK-47 and a nine-millimeter pistol didn't make me feel more secure; I knew that I probably wouldn't survive an IED attack or a heavily armed force all by my lonesome, but I wouldn't be captured, either; I'd go down fighting. Surrendering was a death sentence.

The most dangerous threats on the highway were the insurgents, the Taliban and Al-Qaida warriors. These were the assassins whose objectives were to murder and destroy. And while they weren't above stealing and grabbing whatever prize they could, the road assassins tended to be less entrepreneurial and more sadistic. By killing and destroying, they hoped to discourage others from continuing support of the conflict on their home turf. Thieves and assassins employed similar strategies for taking down their prey, and one of the most popular methods involved burying artillery rounds beneath the highway and electronically detonating them with a cell phone. Another technique involved setting up an ambush by using obstacles: fallen trees or vehicles that appeared to be disabled, for example. In the case of obstacles, as the approaching targets arrived on scene, a barrage of automatic weapon and RPG fire would ensue.

The assassins would also employ suicide bombers driving vehicle-borne improvised explosive devices (VBIED), whereby a sedan full of explosives would pull alongside the target vehicle and detonate. In most cases, the roadway assassins preferred to do their business along the isolated highways. A poorly maintained highway, such as Route Bottle, posed an advantage for the home team, in that it forced travelers to operate their vehicles more slowly, thereby making them easier targets.

My Sunday drive was immediately soured by a convoy of local vehicles moving painfully slow along the rutted highway in front of me. I'd driven the route dozens of times, so I knew the location of every pothole and fissure. I knew it so well that I was able to negotiate the obstacles with the grace of an Olympic skier gliding through the gates of a slalom course. Ahead of me were jingle trucks struggling to achieve speeds more than fifteen mph. The condition of the road was so poor that the big trucks couldn't gain momentum without having to surrender one or more of their wheels to the potholes and crevasses. Adding to the difficulty was the fact that the vehicles were overloaded and dangerously top-heavy. It wasn't uncommon to see a jingle truck lying on its side along the highway. The cargo would be spilled everywhere, and the truck's axles would be twisted from being overstressed by the excessive weight they were trying to haul.

The vehicles in front of me were negotiating the potholes like rhinoceroses performing a ballet. It was ugly. As I approached the small convoy I could see the trouble the jingle trucks were having, traversing across all lanes of the two-way highway while lumbering from side to side like a herd of elephants. Following behind these vehicular mammoths were two Toyota Land Cruiser SUVs, equipped with IED countermeasure antennae. Checking my cell phone, I could see that the countermeasures were active; I'd lost my cell signal and I wouldn't be able to receive or make any phone calls until I could put at least a quarter mile between us.

Both of the SUVs were white with dark, tinted windows. The color of the vehicles, the tinted windows, the countermeasure antennae, and the difficulty with which they were making progress suggested they were up-armored vehicles occupied by Americans. The Americans seem to have an affinity for owning white and black SUVs, so much so that if I had a dollar for every white Toyota Land Cruiser or black Chevy Suburban I encountered in Afghanistan, I could have bailed out Greece.

I exercised caution whenever I came upon a military convoy or a personal service detail (PSD) detachment traveling outside the wire. The occupants onboard tended to be on high alert, and I didn't want to startle anyone by giving an impression that could be perceived as a threat. Civilian contractors rarely drove alone along Afghanistan's remote highways, and once spotted by a convoy's rear turret gunner, a single male (like me) driving a vehicle would be suspect.

Schussing skillfully around potholes enabled me to gain ground, and within minutes I was only several car lengths behind the white Toyota SUVs. I didn't want to make my approach too quickly but I felt confident I had already been seen. Any experienced PSD driver would have noticed me well before I was on their tail. As I approached, they would also notice that I was a single driver.

After reducing the distance between us to no more than two car lengths, I removed my CAC ID from its holder and held it out the window. A US government common access card, or CAC, has a distinct appearance that can be easily recognized, even from a distance. In the past, I had followed many military convoys along the same route, and when I presented my CAC to the rear gunner (stationed atop the last vehicle in the convoy) he or she would use their binoculars to get a better glimpse of my ID card and do a visual scan of my face. Once satisfied, the gunner would give me the thumbs-up signal, which meant I could either overtake the convoy or follow safely in its wake.

As I held my CAC ID out the window, I waited for a sign of acknowledgment from the Toyota in front of me. There was no reaction. I repeated the procedure while flashing my bright lights but got the same results. Next, I tried honking my horn while waving my ID in hopes of getting some attention. Still nothing. *This is starting to get weird,* I thought. After following at such a close distance for nearly two minutes, I couldn't imagine why the vehicle ahead of me had failed to either notice me on his bumper or acknowledge my presence. The driver could have tapped the brake, stuck his arm out the window, or even flipped me the bird. Anything would have sufficed, but to my dismay there was no reaction at all.

"This is strange," I said out loud. "Not good."

I slowed down and backed off five car lengths to reconsider my options. I was only fifteen minutes into my journey and there was still a lot of road ahead of me. I wasn't looking forward to spending my afternoon behind a funeral procession. Scanning the road ahead, I began looking for an opportunity to overtake the lethargic convoy in front of me. Parallel to the highway was a dirt road that ran about ten meters off to the side. My hope was that the Americans would see the road, take it, and pass the jingle trucks in front of them. But the SUVs maintained their course, following the ornate cargo rigs as if they were in no hurry whatsoever.

I was becoming frustrated. We were approaching a notoriously dangerous corridor that was well known for ambushes and attacks, and the vehicles ahead of me were creating a disadvantage for themselves by remaining locked behind the slow-moving convoy. The parallel dirt road provided a route for overtaking the slower vehicles, but if the Americans chose to remain behind the jingle trucks, they would make themselves an easily exploited target. Situating myself behind them placed me at risk as well, and my instincts were telling me to get away from these guys.

After weighing my options, I made my decision: I would pass the entire group by using the parallel dirt road. I calculated that in the event that the SUV occupants had failed to take notice that I was an American, which I doubted, then the distance between the parallel dirt road and the highway should have been sufficient to demonstrate that all I wanted was to pull ahead and be on my way. I was wrong.

After adjusting my seat belt, I placed both hands on the steering wheel and accelerated to gain more speed. In less than three seconds, I had closed the distance to one car length and made a snap turn toward the parallel road. I timed the maneuver perfectly, passing the rear Toyota while angling away from it. Having increased my speed, I was more concerned about losing control of my vehicle than watching the Toyota beside me. Suddenly, I sensed a rapidly approaching object entering into my right peripheral vision. Turning my head just in time, I saw the rear Toyota angling toward the midsection of my vehicle. The other driver was trying to hit me! Instinctively, I floored the accelerator and struggled to maintain control as the rear of my Land Cruiser began to lose traction. While struggling to maintain control, I cursed at the other driver, saying, "What the f**k are you trying to do, kill me?!"

As the rear end of my Toyota slid to the left, I applied correction by steering in the same direction. I was successful in maintaining both control and forward momentum, but not without fishtailing in the opposite direction and throwing a cloud of dust into the air. The commotion I was causing may have looked like a water-skier executing rooster tails, but the water in my wake was actually gravel and dirt spraying high into the air. Meanwhile, the driver of the rear Toyota, who was aiming for me in his heavier yet underpowered vehicle, was less fortunate in establishing the same degree of control. The effect of throwing his steering wheel hard-over while accelerating toward me created a centrifugal force that spun his vehicle in the opposite direction.

In retrospect, the other driver was lucky he didn't roll his top-heavy fortress on wheels. Like me, he tried to compensate by steering in the same direction of his slide, but the conditions he had created were more severe than mine. By stomping on his accelerator and turning into me, he threw himself into a spin—from which he was able to recover—but not without having to pay for his impetuousness with several more fishtails. Had he backed off on the gas, while his vehicle was sliding wildly from side to side, he might have flipped, but to his credit he must have realized his mistake and made the necessary corrections. While he struggled to regain control, I accelerated toward clear air and made my escape.

Escape? Escape from what or whom? Americans? What the hell just happened?

I'm not ashamed to admit that my heart nearly jumped out of my chest as I sped away from the small convoy. Like a fox that had cleverly eluded a pack of clumsy hounds, I didn't lose a second looking back to analyze what had just occurred. I stayed focused on putting distance between my lighter, faster vehicle and the cloud of dust that grew smaller in my rearview mirror.

In December of 2014, journalists Geoff Dyer and Chloe Sorvino, reporting for CNBC, cowrote an article stating that the US had spent

$765 billion on the war in Afghanistan. One hundred billion of the nearly one trillion that was spent was appropriated for reconstruction projects. The War on Terror, which started out as a search and destroy mission against Al-Qaida and the Taliban, had shifted into a nation-building effort for one of poorest countries on Earth.

In terms that might help to describe the war from a nonstrategic perspective, the political objective for Afghanistan was to cure the country of its debilitating condition through the introduction of social inoculations. The injection of financial assistance was akin to pumping antibiotics into a bloodstream inundated by unhealthy cells. The hope was that the remedy might prove effective, whereby a healthier, unified, and independent Afghan society could enjoy a more peaceful existence with itself, while coexisting with the rest of the world through trade and commerce of its vast natural resources.

My colleagues and I, the beneficiaries of this experimental remedy, had frequent discussions of our governments' nation-building strategy. Many of my associates had served in Iraq and witnessed the results of a failed attempt at creating a democratic society in an unwilling culture that was burdened by more problems than the rest of the world was willing to solve. Despite whatever benefits were accrued after receiving even more income-earning opportunities as contractors in Afghanistan, the Iraq War contractors were justifiably baffled by the US government's second attempt at trying to create democracy—under worse conditions!

Comparatively speaking, Afghanistan is a far less advanced society than Iraq, but for the rest of us who weren't afforded the firsthand education that our Iraqi contractor vets experienced, we saw the political strategies as flawed as well. Afghanistan was receiving billions of dollars in financial support without any requirement on the part of the local populace to reciprocate or redeem themselves. Efforts to eliminate the Taliban and Al-Qaida, develop a national infrastructure, build schools, and establish a national (Afghan) security force were aimed at providing Afghanistan with the baseline it would need to live in peace, advance as a culture, and protect itself from future threats. Few people disagreed with the merits of such a strategy, but the political doctors prescribing Afghanistan's socioeconomic inoculations failed to take into account several preexisting conditions. First, Afghanistan wasn't ready for democracy; it's a country ruled by tribal law. Second, and because Afghanistan is ruled by tribal law, rewiring the population's mind-set toward socioeconomic independence, self-reliance, and the development of democratic practices would take generations.

Finally (and here's where we uttered the three magic words while seeing firsthand the fruitless results of a limited war effort in lieu of a nation-building program), the American taxpayers weren't willing to finance such an experiment during one of the worst economic periods in US history. America had its own problems.

Daniel Trotta, correspondent and journalist for Reuters, wrote an article published in March of 2014 stating that the war in Iraq had cost the US $1.6 trillion with an additional $490 billion in benefits owed to war veterans. Trotta didn't mention the number of US casualties sustained during the conflict, so I conducted my own research. The US Department of Defense casualty website reported 4,425 KIA (killed in action, hostile and nonhostile) and 32,223 wounded during Operation Iraqi Freedom. Trotta's article quoted Steven Bucci, who served as a military assistant to former defense secretary Donald Rumsfeld. Bucci said, "If we had had the foresight to see how long it [the war in Iraq] would last and even if it would have cost half the lives, we would not have gone in."

Unlike the war in Iraq, the US military didn't target and destroy government buildings throughout Afghanistan; we weren't at war with the Afghan military or their government. While pursuing the Taliban, the US and its coalition forces certainly leveled more than a few villages, but the major cities remained intact. One has to wonder, therefore, why all the fuss over "rebuilding" Afghanistan to the tune of $100 billion? I could be wrong, but doesn't the term "rebuild" apply to the construction of something that had previously existed? During the war in Iraq, power plants, bridges, and key government buildings were destroyed and subsequently rebuilt. The US also helped to re-build Germany and Japan after the Second World War. Conversely, the majority of the US and NATO-funded projects in Afghanistan were dedicated to the creation of infrastructure and assets that never existed.

America and its coalition partners weren't following the same (flawed) strategy that had been employed in Iraq; the money being spent was akin to dumping truckloads of coins into a wishing well, in hopes of improving one's chances for a miracle. Spending tens of thousands of dollars on quick picks to narrow the odds of winning a $100 million state lottery would have made more sense. After the war in Iraq and all of its failed strategies, I wondered why anyone would believe the results in Afghanistan would be any different. All indicators that such a strategy would fail (again) were staring us right in the face.

Whiskey, Tango, Foxtrot.

I've spoken about the airfield projects requiring sand, gravel, and concrete to construct the building foundations and air operating surfaces that my employers were producing in the previous chapter, and how the process of transferring material over the fence mitigated the security threats. When I proposed the idea to the officer-in-charge (OIC) of base security, he embraced it from the standpoint that any truck that never left the base was a truck that didn't pose a threat. The concept was similar to a passenger who passes through airport security. Once passengers clear security—and as long as they remain inside the airport—they're no longer viewed as a potential threat. The base security officer also concluded that time and money saved by the contractor created a benefit that could be transferred to the warfight-ers, who would receive a promptly completed project sooner.

When we first developed the idea of sending concrete over the perimeter fence, the concept was far from being considered normal. Once the over-the-fence operations were approved, however, it set the stage for a new way of doing business between our company and the soldiers who were responsible for the physical security of the base. We knew the consideration we had earned came with greater responsibility to demonstrate strict compliance within the special conditions that had been extended—but in return, we hoped to earn the confidence of our military partners and their respect. With that, our ability to build (without delay) would most certainly be enhanced. Time was money, so the development of a better relationship with the military was paramount. Having been granted special access to provide concrete over the fence indicated to the Turks that they weren't being treated like any ordinary firm, they were being given special consideration. Sadly, this was not the case at all.

After sundown, the entry control points were secured and all traffic coming in and out of the base was suspended until the next morning. Late one night, a worker from our concrete batch plant (on the other side of the perimeter fence) woke up with severe chest pains. In the hope of receiving some medical assistance from the US military, the man was escorted to the ECP by several of his colleagues. Having arrived at the gate two hours before its scheduled opening, however, the men were denied access—including the man who was doubled over in pain. Despite their pleas, none of the gate guards could be persuaded to notify their supervisor for assistance or request medical aid for the man in pain.

The soldiers working the gate stood their ground, refusing to deviate from what they believed were orders that offered no leeway. Their job was to maintain security and open the gate at its prescribed time. Subsequently, and after enduring excruciating pain for over an hour, the worker collapsed and lost consciousness. Fearing that the man was in fact quite ill, the soldiers opened the gate and arranged for transportation to the base hospital. By this time, however, it was too late. The man was dead.

I received the details of what had occurred over the phone. As I sat there listening, I was speechless. I didn't get angry, I didn't yell, and I didn't say a word; I simply hung up the phone and remained quiet for a few minutes. There are times in life when words simply cannot describe how a person feels, and that was one of them.

Looking back, I recognize that the man was just another casualty of war. The soldiers mistakenly believed that following orders superseded the need to think outside the box. In retrospect, I'm reminded that life is about managing priorities, and while there are times when certain people fail to grasp that concept, it doesn't excuse them from failing to do what they should have or could have. Being deployed in a war zone took its toll on everyone; it exposed the worst in all of us. Surviving the day-to-day challenges was an effort all by itself, but whenever we were forced to deal with unprofessional, insensitive, or stupid people, all it did was make matters worse.

By 2012, it became clear to my colleagues and me that the US government wasn't pursuing victory in Afghanistan. We understood that winning the war would require more killing and more money than the US government, NATO, and the media that influenced public opinion were willing to justify. The US and its coalition forces' superior technology had the capability to seek out and destroy the enemy—but their hands were tied; the politicians on Capitol Hill were afraid of the media's reaction to the collateral damage that would ensue. When news broke that the US and its coalition forces would withdraw from Afghanistan, few people even took notice; they were distracted by more topical headlines:

Whitney Houston Dies of a Fatal Drug Overdose
Justin Bieber Arrested for DUI

It was depressing to note that the headlines commanded more attention than the stories that were no longer being reported. Dying on the field of battle in the fight to defeat global terrorism was old news; nobody was interested anymore. In an attempt to honor his campaign promise, President Obama justified the exodus of US forces, claiming the mission had been a success; American troops had outfitted and trained Afghan security forces to protect and defend their own country. Within two years of the troop drawdown however, the situation in Afghanistan began to deteriorate as Taliban forces resumed their former occupation.

On October 15, 2015, President Obama reported to the nation his revised strategy for Afghanistan: "In key areas of the country, the security situation is still very fragile, and in some places there is risk of deterioration." President Obama ended his speech by stating what he felt was a need to maintain a higher concentration of US troops through 2017.

By all accounts, life in Afghanistan was returning to normal: everything was going to hell.

CHAPTER TEN

R&R: The Joy and Heartaches of Reconnecting

N othing quite surpassed the anticipation of leaving the battlefield and taking some well-deserved time off. Contractors were entitled to take R&R after two to six months in theater, depending on which company they worked for and the type of job they had. The higher-risk jobs typically offered more frequent breaks, thereby allowing people to reenergize and return to work properly rested.

The longer a person stayed in theater without a break, the more prone they became to hitting the wall. "The wall" was the point where people became intolerant, less effective on the job, anxious, and near their breaking point. I'd hit my wall after being away from home for a period of three to four months.

Early into my first assignment, I got tied up with several projects that kept me in theater for over five months. As my leave date grew closer, Barbara and I started planning our long-overdue reunion. Having set up home in Bahrain meant that we were only hours away from one of my bucket list destinations: Egypt. Since boyhood, I had always wanted to see the pyramids and explore the many wonders of

Egypt's ancient civilization. After serving months in captivity, I was also looking forward to a relaxing vacation. *Is that possible in Egypt?* I wondered. I would soon find out.

Barbara, who had visited Cairo many years before we met, told me about the Mena House Oberoi, an incredible hotel on the outskirts of Cairo, right next to the Great Pyramid. Built in the late 1800s as a hunting resort, the Mena House served as headquarters to the British Army during the Second World War and was later transformed into five-star resort. While researching the hotel on the internet, I was impressed by its splendor, historical significance, and proximity to the Giza pyramids.

Barbara, bless her heart, found a three-star all-inclusive hotel located only a mile from the pyramids. She was pleased with what she'd found, a bargain-hunter's dream and a fine hotel indeed. Having hit my wall over a month before, I was in already in a less than desirable state, to say the least.

"I don't want to stay at some three-star bargain-basement hotel, Barb," I announced into the phone. "We're staying at the Mena House. I checked it out on the internet, and that's where I want to stay. Call the travel agent and tell him we're switching to the Mena House—and book us a room with *pyramid* view."

"The Mena House is too expensive," Barbara protested politely, trying to remain patient. "We don't need to stay at such an expensive hotel, the other place will be fine."

"C'mon, Barb," I replied. "This will probably be the only time we ever go to Egypt, and I want to make the most of it. Cancel the reservations you made at the other place, and book us at the Mena—please."

Barbara persisted: "What's wrong with you? I found us a very good deal and I'm trying to save money."

"What's wrong?" I replied, feeling myself starting to shudder like a Saturn rocket whose boosters had just been ignited and was about to blast off from the launchpad. "I'll tell you what's the matter. I'm tired of being out here, and the last thing I need is an argument from you over the cost of a hotel that I can well afford."

Photo from author's collection.

Liftoff, we have liftoff! Apollo 13 has cleared the tower and is rocketing skyward on its epic journey to the moon!

Barbara went silent. Sensing I'd gone too far, I took a breath.

"Look, Barb, I've been waiting a long time for this vacation. I want it to be comfortable and relaxing. The Mena House costs more money 'cause it's way nicer. Let's do this, okay? Trust me, you're going to love it."

Our vacation to Egypt was my first R&R from Afghanistan, and the beginning of what would become an extravagant trend that Barbara neither expected nor felt comfortable with, at least not at first. I was the one who engineered the policy of pulling out all the stops and having the best of everything whenever we went on holiday, and I did so because I felt as though we had earned it: being apart from one another for several months at a time warranted special treatment. My justifications included noting that people got killed in my line of work. There was no telling whether this would be my last vacation on Earth, so I thought, let's live it up and have fun! I was also cognizant of the fact that there was a limited amount of time for me to enjoy the fruits of this unique opportunity. I wouldn't be earning that kind of money forever, and I wanted to enjoy it while it lasted.

When we arrived at the Mena House, it was more spectacular than Barbara and I had imagined. After the bellman escorted us to our room, however, I looked out the window to discover that our accommodations did not include a view of the pyramids but a garden in the back of the hotel. Irritated, yet trying to remain calm, I turned to Barbara and asked why I was looking at *trees* instead of *pyramids*.

"This will be fine," she said. "It's a beautiful room, don't you think?"

"Yes, it's a nice room—but it's not what we asked for," I replied.

I was disappointed by the fact that our vacation had just started and I was already feeling dissatisfied. I instructed the bellman to stand fast while I rang up the front desk and requested (very firmly) that we be placed in another room—with a *pyramid* view, as our reservation had guaranteed.

Looking back, I was quite the pill throughout the first half of our Egyptian holiday, but the moment of truth came while shopping at the Grand Souk in downtown Cairo. The aisles were packed with tourist trinkets and souvenirs, and to my frustration the local merchants were pestering us to make a purchase. After ten minutes of repetitive "No, thank you...we're just looking...I'm sorry, not today" responses (and receiving indignant looks in return), I'd had enough; I was ready to leave.

"Can we go now, Barb?" I moaned, walking away from a ripe-smelling merchant who was unsuccessfully trying to draw my attention to a collection of scarabs and King Tut statues.

"These people are poor, Kevin," Barbara sighed. "They rely on tourists to make their living."

I should have taken note of Barbara trying to be patient with me, but I wasn't paying attention. I was caught up in my own drama.

"I see poverty and sadness every day in Afghanistan, Barbara," I quipped. "I don't want to have to deal with it while I'm on vacation, okay? Besides," I continued, "I'd probably buy something if these guys would just give us a little space."

Just then, a young Egyptian merchant stepped in front of me and placed a souvenir statue of Ramses in my face.

"How about this, my friend?" said the young man, full of enthusiasm. "I give you good price—very cheap."

I glared at the young man with contempt. If my eyes had been daggers, he would have been skewered.

"Hey, bud," I replied slowly to the young man. I was in no mood for diplomacy, and my tone was very clear. "You need to get the hell out of my way, okay?"

The young merchant stared back at me, wide-eyed and slack-jawed. Slowly, he stepped aside. I could see that he was embarrassed, but I was less concerned for his feelings than my desire to reacquire my personal space and resume my exit toward the parking lot. I felt bad for a split second, but relieved that our encounter had ended before it even began.

"Are you happy now?" Barbara snapped with disappointment. "You broke that boy's heart."

"Haven't you figured out yet that I've had enough of this place?" I barked back. Sweat running down my back had caused my shirt to stick to me, and I was starting to get a headache.

"What's the matter with you, Kevin?" she replied with harsh disappointment.

Barbara's patience was gone, and her enthusiasm for our trip to the Souk had been deflated by my uncooperative demeanor. The tone of her voice suggested both confusion and frustration. She was enjoying the experience of shopping at the Souk, as well as her interaction with the merchants who were driving me crazy; I was ready to kill the next guy who tried to force me into smelling a bottle of knockoff perfume. *No thanks, man, I'm good.*

Making matters worse, Barbara would stop, sample the perfume, and then decide she didn't want to buy anything. *Thanks, Barb. Now you can deal with the guy who's tailgating us!*

"Come...look...I make discount...half-price!" the merchants would plead.

I was miserable, and I wanted to go back to the hotel. Barbara dug in her purse, pulled out some coins, and handed them to the young man who I had insulted. We took a taxi back to the hotel. Barbara wasn't happy with me and I was feeling like a complete ass. Our dream vacation wasn't turning out as either of us had planned.

In the years to come, I became keenly aware that working in Afghanistan had changed me. I think it changed most everyone who spent time downrange; you can't live in a war zone without being affected in some way, and in most cases the changes weren't positive.

Vacations from the war zone became the contractors' way of coping with what they would eventually return to: austere living conditions, isolation from family and friends, and the threat of an unscheduled trip to the hospital or cemetery. Combating such conditions wasn't difficult; all one needed was a healthy distraction. Something as simple as showing up to work in color-coordinated cargo pants, shirt, and bandanna worked for some people, while others took to pimping out their living quarters with all the comforts of home: flat-screen TVs, Xbox game ensembles, and an assortment of comfort food and snacks purchased online. Even the smallest reminders of a normal life could make living behind the wire feel just like home. Whatever it was that distracted people from the day-to-day grind of working twelve- to sixteen-hour days served as a prelude to the ultimate distraction of all, taking leave.

While on vacation from the war zone, most contractors flew home, hung out around the house, had cookouts with family and friends, or took side trips to popular points of interest, such as Disney World and Hawaii. Some folks went on cruises, while others vacationed at more elaborate destinations, such as Europe or the Caribbean. Upon their return, people shared photos of the time they spent with their families, and it was pleasing to see people return to work rejuvenated, and ready to take on another three to four months in the box.

One of my favorite R&R stories was told to me by a former British special forces operator by the name of Del. Del was a regular guy, soft-spoken and never one to brag. After leaving the SAS, he served as a hired gun for a private security outfit that supported the company I worked with during my last tour of duty. I was glad to have Del on our team. We had jobsites in some of the most dangerous parts of Afghanistan, and the protection he offered encompassed years of military training and combat experience. Del carried a cache of weapons and ammunition on him at all times, and he had a backup arsenal in the trunk of his SUV. He was loaded for bear.

While supporting a project in Delaram, a group of us swapped stories about where we'd been on vacation. Del told us about the time he dropped over $23,000 for a two-week stay at the Burj Al Arab Hotel in Dubai. The Burj is an international icon, a world-famous luxury hotel that resembles a large white sail on a man-made island off Jumeirah Beach. It's been voted the most luxurious hotel in the world for several years running. Every room is a suite, and the guests are treated to unparalleled service that includes butlers, in-room chefs, masseuses, and much more.

I, too, had spent some money while on R&R, but nothing compared to what Del had laid out at the Burj. For Barbara's birthday, one year, I made reservations at one of our favorite dining establishments in Dubai, Armani Ristorante, located within the Armani Hotel at the Burj Al Khalifa, the tallest building in the world. On the night of Barbara's birthday, the staff was waiting for us with flowers, chocolates, and champagne at our table, which overlooked the Dubai Fountains. Throughout the multicourse meal, the head chef, Alessandro, made several visits to our table with samples of delicacies prepared by his crew of Italian apprentices. Barbara and I wined and dined for several hours, and when our evening was concluded I paid an obscene amount of money for the dinner tab and left a hefty gratuity for our servers. It was a win-win for all parties concerned; Barbara's birthday was a success, and the Armani staff went home with a nice tip.

When I shared the $1,235.00 dinner receipt with my pals back in Afghanistan, hands were slapping the breakfast table in astonishment, along with a flurry of apropos expletives. If memory serves me correctly, the actual words expressed by the phonetic meaning of *Whiskey, Tango, Foxtrot* were spoken with vigor.

Back in Delaram, I was equally amazed by Del's story. "I've spent some money on vacations in my day," I admitted to Del, "but I don't know if I could drop that kind of dough."

Del paused for a moment and looked at me with the seriousness of a courtroom judge. He said, "I served in both Gulf Wars and survived more times than I should have. I'm living on borrowed time, so I just figured, what the hell."

Borrowed time. Now there was a concept for consideration. Del's synopsis captured the essence of what a lot of us were feeling but few of us could articulate. A surprising number of people I worked with agreed that living and working at the lowest levels of life's comfort zone warranted treating ourselves while on R&R. In effect, our rest periods away from the war zone could be described as "living the dream."

One of the advantages of having a job on the other side of the world was that contractors had easy access to exotic destinations. Trips to the Middle East, Europe, and even the Far East were often half the distance to Middle America. Setting up house in Bahrain reduced the burden of traveling home from Afghanistan, and let's face it, there's nothing fun or exciting about flying aboard a commercial aircraft these days. The low cost of air travel means more people have access to flying on planes than ever before. I'm not a big fan of crowds, so I avoid going to places such as amusement parks and concerts. One of my objectives while on leave was to isolate myself from the masses. To accomplish this, I tried to place myself where most people couldn't afford to go. Having a job that provided me with the resources to exercise such options was an advantage, and I used it as often as I could.

For Barbara's birthday, one year, I took her to Paris. We had visited Paris several times in the past, but for this trip I wanted to pull out all the stops. I made reservations at an upscale hotel near the Louvre Museum, we saw everything Paris has to offer, and dined to our hearts' content.

Paris is a spectacular vacation destination, but the downside is that sixteen million tourists per year have come to the same conclusion—which is great for the French economy—but not so great for people like me who hate crowds. Knowing that my preference for avoiding the masses wouldn't be possible, I calculated that avoiding the throngs was still doable. All I had to do was stick to my plan: avoid public transportation by using taxis, and be willing to pay the price for higher-end services.

Like most of the vacation plans I concocted, many of which took place in my eight-by-twenty container during a midnight rocket attack, my overly ambitious plan for a peaceful vacation in Paris went out the window within minutes of arriving, thanks to my thrifty wife. Our trip began by flying into Charles de Gaulle International Airport and taking a train to the heart of the city. From *le gare* (the train station), we needed to make our way to our hotel on the Rue de Rivoli, a main boulevard that passes right in front of the Louvre. Having been to Paris several times before, Barbara thought she had a pretty good

Photo from author's collection.

grasp of the lay of the land. Much to my chagrin, however, her land navigation skills left something to be desired. As we rolled our luggage out of the station, I began to look for a taxi.

The birthday girl had other plans. While I was looking around for a cab, she whipped out her well-used tourist map, the one she had saved from our previous trips.

"We can walk to the hotel from here," Barbara said, pointing to her map with confidence. "Look, it's not that far away."

Crap! We just got here, and my plans are going south already!

Not wanting to spoil her enthusiasm, I conceded. The sun was shining and besides, this was *her* birthday adventure. *Be patient,* I thought to myself. *How bad could it be?*

Forty minutes and six kilometers later, we arrived at our hotel. Barbara was all smiles, still fresh as a daisy, having dragged her lightweight carry-on behind her. I hadn't fared as well. Our death march through hordes of tourists and city traffic rendered my well-groomed appearance into a grotesque figure that resembled the Hunchback of Notre Dame, bent over in pain while dragging two oversized suitcases behind him.

By the afternoon of our second day, I was spent; my feet were killing me, and I was tired of being around so many people. For the better part of two days, I had tolerated being pushed, stepped on, and bumping nuts-to-butts into more strangers than I care to admit. The irrepressible Barbara, however, was still marching forward like a tour guide on a mission.

"Ke..." (*Italian: Kev*). Barbara was urging me to step up the pace from her position ten feet in front of me. "Our next stop is the Eiffel Tower."

"I can't go any further, Barb," I protested, stopping in the middle of the street, hoping to be run over by a Parisian driving a Peugeot. "I'm done."

"Vieni!" (*Italian: Come on!*). Barbara walked to where I was standing, took hold of my forearm, and led me to the curb. "It's not that far... look!" she cajoled. "I can see it from here!"

"The Eiffel Tower is nearly a thousand feet tall, Goddammit!" I protested. "You can see it from anywhere in the city! If you want to go to the Eiffel Tower, then let me get a cab!"

So much for diplomacy. Barbara wrinkled her nose as she looked off into the distance at the iron spire. As she altered her focus back to her map, she shook her head in disgust.

Oh no, she's looking for another attraction—something closer!

Thinking quickly, I decided to change tactics.

"Why don't we take a little rest?" I suggested.

Barbara didn't offer a response while studying her map.

"Barb, it's after four. We've been at this all day. Let's grab a seat at this café and have a glass of wine."

Reluctantly, Barbara conceded. She was tired from all the walking as well, but her sense of adventure wouldn't permit her to acknowledge defeat. Folding her map, she placed it back in her purse and studied the layout of the café next to where we were standing. Having warmed up to the idea of some refreshment, and a break from pounding the pavement (she mentioned to me earlier that her feet were starting to ache), she headed for the ladies' room while I hailed a waiter and asked to see a menu. I speak very little French, but I'm familiar with their wine, so I made a quick selection and ordered a bottle of Pouilly-Fumé. By the time Barbara returned, our waiter had already worked his magic: the wine, two glasses, and an assortment of cheese and crackers were waiting on our table.

As the waiter pulled the bottle from the wine chiller and presented one of Barbara's favorite labels to her for inspection (as directed) she seemed to forget about the Eiffel Tower and all the other attractions we had failed to see that day. Forty-five minutes later, the Pouilly-Fumé had been drained and the assortment of cheese and crackers had been reduced to crumbs. Between the refreshments and a lovely Parisian sunset along the Champs-Élysées, Barbara lost her desire to see just one more attraction before calling it a day. As we headed back to the hotel in our taxi, I was thinking to myself, *I need to get back to Afghanistan—for some rest and relaxation!*

Taking leave came with its share of challenges. For starters, the contractor often left the battlefield with a head full of stress. Upon returning home, there would be an adjustment period: catching up on some well-deserved rest and spending the next few days trying to find the balance between adjusting to the real world and accommodating everyone else's agenda—which didn't always align with what the contractor had in mind—could be a challenge in itself.

During the onset of my contracting career, I took several trips to California to visit my family. To save money, Barbara and I flew economy class. As I explained earlier, I'm not exactly *petite* so by the end of the twenty-plus-hour journey, I felt as though I'd been through hell and back. I've never been able to sleep much on airplanes and traveling to the other side of the world took three to four days to adjust. By the time I felt rested, there were but a handful of days to actually enjoy myself, and then it was time to leave again. So much for a restful holiday.

All other disappointments aside, and as an expat who chose to live outside the US while working in the war zone, I found it increasingly difficult to justify those long trips to California. The level of effort combined with the difficulty in trying to satisfy so many objectives (within a compressed time frame) wasn't cutting it; there wasn't enough time for me to accomplish everything I had hoped to achieve. My to-do list was long and far too ambitious considering the fact that first and foremost, I needed some well-deserved rest and relaxation. Flying home from Afghanistan and then jumping on a thirteen-hour flight put a dent in that plan. Spending time with my parents and siblings (which I enjoyed immensely) didn't allow for much of the one-on-one time that Barbara and I desired, but she understood and received the same consideration from me whenever we visited her family in Italy.

During my visits to California, I felt obliged to try and reconnect with my estranged children. Since I moved overseas, we'd grown further and further apart. I missed the baseball games, school functions, interface with the kids' friends, etc. If you can name an event that included kids spending time with their parents, I can assure you I wasn't there for it. As a parent, knowing my kids were growing up without me was heartbreaking. What I came to realize was that, over time, life itself provided a remedy. You may recall reading the section where I wrote that absence doesn't guarantee that the heart will grow fonder. There's another saying that warrants mentioning as well: *out of sight, out of mind*. In other words, even a broken heart can mend. I'm not saying my children and I were pleased or comfortable with the outcome that transpired, I'm simply saying we adjusted. Life went on.

The challenges associated with being disassociated were complicated and hard to manage. I wasn't alone in my struggle, however; I had company. I heard similar stories from colleagues who, like me, had been away from their families for so long they'd become strangers in their own homes. The problem with being away for so long is that life moves on. The absence of a spouse, parent, or significant other resulted in couples and children gravitating in directions that varied or conflicted with whatever programs existed while the downrange loved one was living at home. These changes didn't occur overnight, they happened over time. Losing touch and being relegated to second-class citizenship within one's own family were common symptoms of a condition I was fond of describing as *Contractoritis*, a term I coined while in Afghanistan.

Contractoritis doesn't exist in any medical journals, but it's a real condition that affected literally thousands of civilian contractors. Here is a list of some of the symptoms:

- Developing a certain level of comfort under the worst of conditions, e.g., sharing a tent with nine other people and thinking to yourself, *This isn't so bad.*
- Believing that living in a wooden-framed plywood B-Hut was equivalent to "Movin' On Up" with George and Louise Jefferson. You'd hit the lottery. No more tent!
- After finally acquiring a twenty-foot container with a private bathroom and shower, you pimp it out with a flat-screen TV

and Xbox and build shelves to hold all the snacks and other paraphernalia purchased from Amazon.com.

- Acquiring your own private hooch (with private bath and shower) felt like five-star living. In reality, it was still an eight-by-twenty-foot box that was subject to being shot at by rockets and mortars—while the wife and kids lived at home in a nice house and drove the new car you had purchased for them—and you didn't seem to mind.

- You were actually hoping for a follow-on contract. Having beaten the odds thus far (you hadn't been killed—yet—and you still had all your fingers and toes), and after making good with creditors who hounded you night and day last year, you're still not satisfied; you want more. With only a few years left before the second trust deed on your house is paid off, you're actually hoping to stay downrange for another year, instead of throwing in the towel and quitting while you're ahead.

- Your wife and kids have developed an insatiable appetite for demanding more stuff—elaborate vacations, private trainers, karate lessons...the list goes on and on—and yet, whenever you Skype back home, someone always seems to have a complaint that requires your intervention.

The list above consists of but a few symptoms of Contractoritis, the condition whereby both the contractor and his/her family have become blinded by a false sense of perpetual good fortune and misguided satisfaction as a result of living separate lives.

A colleague (whom I'll call Tim) married a Malaysian woman with whom he was head over heels in love. He spoiled her by providing her with a generous allowance that enabled her to provide sustenance for herself—and members of her family. Tim talked a good game about his plans to retire from Afghanistan and open a bar on the beach.

One day, he came to work looking glum. When we asked Tim why, he seemed upset. He said his wife had called him, asking for more money each month. Recounting his story to us, Tim asked his wife, "Why do you need more money? Don't I provide you with enough money each month?"

"Yes, honey," his wife replied. "But I need to start saving money for our divorce."

"Divorce?" Tim replied in confusion. "What are you talking about? We were just married six months ago. Why would you say such a thing? I thought we were happy together. Aren't we?"

"Sure," Tim's wife replied. "But eventually everyone gets divorced, and I need to start planning for my future."

Whiskey, Tango, Foxtrot.

Despite the fact that Barbara and I spent many years apart, we were never actually that far from one another. The Kingdom of Bahrain is but a half-day's journey from Afghanistan, which made it both handy and convenient when I had the opportunity to go home. Having Barbara living close to where I worked also provided a measure of relief. Barbara lived alone, so if she ever needed my assistance, I felt comfortable knowing I could get to her fairly quickly.

While driving our Land Rover SUV to the supermarket one day, Barbara noticed smoke starting to seep through the air-conditioning vents. By the time she pulled into a nearby parking lot, smoke had filled the interior of the car and flames were licking out from under the hood. Within minutes, the vehicle was engulfed in flames and was a total loss. Fortunately, Barbara escaped without injury. The cause of the fire turned out to be a faulty wiring harness. The Land Rover dealership that sold us the car had neglected to notify us of a factory recall item that warranted a visit to the shop for repairs. Within a couple of days, I flew home to Bahrain and purchased another vehicle, a Jeep Wrangler Sahara that Barbara named *Penelope.*

Throughout much of the time I spent in Afghanistan, I rented a villa so that Barbara could establish residence in a safe and comfortable community. Having spent time with me while I was stationed in Bahrain during the war, Barbara came to know the island well. Like a cold-blooded reptile, Barbara moves best when her core temperature is warm. She also felt safe among the Bahrainis (who are extremely kind and hospitable) and was comforted by the fact that she could navigate in her Jeep through the capital city of Manama with little difficulty.

Photos from author's collection.

Bahrain is quite liberal, by Muslim standards. The dress code for women calls for covering up shoulders and legs, but expat women are given a pass. Alcohol is sold at hotels and certain restaurants, nightclubs offer entertainment into the wee hours of morning, and prostitution is rampant. Bahrain offers so much in terms of entertainment that its neighbors from Saudi Arabia, Kuwait, and Qatar are frequent visitors—every weekend, in fact.

Despite all that Bahrain had to offer, Barbara chose to lead a sheltered life. She did her shopping every day to acquire fresh food for her healthy diet, laid out by the pool after lunch, and worked out at the gym I set up in one of the spare bedrooms. After her workout, Barbara would shower, prepare dinner, and watch TV. We brought our Sky TV cable box from Italy so she could monitor the Italian news broadcasts and watch her home improvement shows, dubbed in Italian. During the week, and on weekends, Barbara stayed home in the evenings. She didn't have many friends, but she never felt alone. Barbara is a creature of habit; she has her routines, and she's comfortable doing the same thing every day. She was also cognizant of the fact that socializing among other people might increase the odds for being placed in situations she would rather avoid.

I respected Barbara's self-discipline and loyalty, to the extent that I followed suit. I never frequented a club in Dubai, nor went out drinking with the guys at Kabul's expat watering holes: The Sizzler, Serena Hotel, or the Intercontinental. I drank while I was downrange; I'm not denying that. But I never drank where I wasn't supposed to, nor frequented a club or a lounge. I didn't have the desire nor the bandwidth to engage in activities that could potentially undermine the integrity of my marriage, or the professional relationship I had earned with my employers.

When I finally arrived home on leave, it felt as though a great weight had been lifted; I felt free and happy. It took a couple of days before I could rid myself of that tendency to look over my shoulder, or ignore the random sounds of the city that resembled the crack of a rifle or the growl of a distant explosion. After a good night's sleep in my own bed, I felt well rested and refreshed.

As was customary, whenever I was home I conducted a perfunctory inspection of the premises to ensure that everything was in good working order. I checked the oil in the car and gave it a thorough washing, looking for any new dents or scratches that may have been made while I was away. Whenever we went out, Barbara let me drive her beloved Penelope. Barbara had a habit of providing me with the navigation she thought I needed. Whether we drove to the shopping mall (a half hour away) or to the supermarket (just five minutes down the road) Barbara was on point, telling me which lane I needed to be in, and whether or not the coast was clear to make a turn. Whenever I was behind the wheel it felt as though I was a student driver all over again, but I let it slide. Barbara and Penelope were like a couple of girl-friends who didn't approve of boys entering their clubhouse.

While en route to the supermarket, one day, Barbara was in clas-sic form. "Get into that lane over there," she said, pointing down the street. "You have to turn left at the signal."

"Uh...I think I know where I'm going, Barb. We've lived here for five years, petunia."

Unfazed by my ability to successfully navigate city streets within a mile of our home, Barbara proceeded to monitor my course correc-tions as if the precision of my driving would determine whether or not we could make that kill shot on the Death Star. As we entered the parking lot, her eyes narrowed. She scanned for an open stall.

"Park over there, that's my spot," she directed.

"Take it easy, Barb. I got this," I said, trying to remain patient.

"What are you doing?" she asked as I cruised slowly past "her spot," which in my view posed a risk of sustaining door strikes from two banged-up vehicles that were parked adjacent to the empty space.

"There's my spot right there...go back!" she gasped.

As if the volume had been muted, I glided peacefully past Barbara's selected parking stall, to what I perceived as a more desirable location. Everything was going in slow motion: Barbara's astonishment mir-rored the US media's reaction to Donald Trump's presidential defeat over Hillary Clinton. Horror. Social meltdown. The end of civilization.

"Ke—where are you going! You drove right by that empty spot!" Gliding our Jeep Wrangler into another empty stall (four parking spaces away), I threw the car into park and smiled smugly at my ir-ritated passenger.

"Barb," I explained calmly, "that spot was too narrow. I chose this one so our car wouldn't get scratched. Look, there's no one around us. No one will ever scratch the car out here."

"We're ten kilometers away from the store," she replied sarcastically.

"Come on, my love," I replied as I exited the car, dismissing her sarcasm. "Let's see if they have my favorite Cheetos."

As the above story displays, the first couple of days at home tended to be a bit tense. Going on R&R provided relief from the peculiarities of living in a war zone but that didn't relieve me from respecting the routines that existed at home; routines that were oftentimes forgotten as a result of being away for so long. Oftentimes, therefore, readjusting to life on the home front (where someone else besides me was accustomed to being in charge all the time) required patience and finesse. The odds for a smooth transition were minimized whenever I came home bearing gifts. I learned a long time ago that it didn't take a great deal of effort to please Barbara, so whenever I could demonstrate that she was in my thoughts while we were apart, it paid dividends. Each time I came home, therefore, I arrived with all kinds of trinkets: tablecloths and handmade items I had purchased from the Afghan markets and bazaars, necklaces and bracelets made with lapis lazuli, and a menagerie of knickknacks from the duty-free shop in Dubai: a coffee mug showing all the tourists attractions, a large bag of pistachio nuts, a package of dates, and my signature gifts, which consisted of the same two items I brought home each time I returned from Afghanistan: a Hermes silk scarf for Barbara and a bottle of Dom Pérignon champagne to celebrate our reunion.

My policy of never arriving home empty-handed added to the flavor of a happy homecoming. It wasn't necessary or expected, but let's face it: everyone likes to receive gifts, especially from exotic locations. Many of the things I brought home were regifted to members of the family and friends who were equally excited to receive something from so unique a place as Arabia and Afghanistan.

When we arrived home from the supermarket, it was late afternoon. After hauling all the groceries into the kitchen, I started putting everything away in the cupboards and the refrigerator.

"Go watch TV, I'll do this," Barbara said, waving me away.

"I can help," I replied unenthusiastically. I knew she didn't need my help. I was simply putting up a front. What I really wanted to do was lie on the sofa, watch TV, and eventually nod off to sleep. I had thought often about enjoying this moment while in Afghanistan, and I was eager to start checking off those boxes from my R&R to-do list. Barbara, who, like all wives, has extrasensory perception and voodoo powers that can render their husbands defenseless, knew I was up to something besides spending time with her. Looking at me over the top of her reading glasses, she gave me a fake smile but said nothing.

"Okay," I conceded. *Message received, I'm not fooling her.* "I've got an idea..." I was trying to sound diplomatic while realizing the ruse had not worked. "I'm going to lie down on the sofa and watch some TV."

Shortly after settling into my domain, Barbara brought me a glass of wine and my beloved Cheetos, the big, fat, fluffy ones.

"I'm going upstairs to take a shower," she said, putting her cheek next to mine so I could give her a kiss. As she walked up the stairs, she reminded me of the evening's itinerary: "We're going to dinner at 8:30, so don't fall asleep."

"Yes, dear."

"And don't touch my sofa with your Cheeto fingers," she added.

"Roger that," I replied, brushing the Cheetos dust off my shirt and cringing as the little orange crumbs fell onto the couch.

Several hours later, I was startled from my nap by the sound of Barbara calling to me from upstairs. Mummified beneath a blanket, I hadn't moved a hair since falling into my couch coma. My eyes began to refocus as I scanned my surroundings. *Where am I?* Suddenly it became clear: *I'm not in my container...and I'm not in Afghanistan. I'm at home, lying on my couch. Sweet!*

"*Forza!*" Barbara shouted from upstairs. (*Italian: Get going, move it!*)

"Okay," I yelled, shaking the cobwebs from my head as I attempted to stand up.

As I made my way up the stairs, I spied Barbara traversing across the upstairs atrium into the other bedroom where her clothes were kept. We had four bedrooms with full bathrooms on the second story, and she chose to use one of the bathrooms as her private space. I had the master bathroom to myself, and as I bounded up the stairs I noticed that all she was wearing were a pair of flip-flops, her bra, and a thong.

Note to self: Don't drink too much tonight. You might fall asleep and miss the big event.

Batman would have been impressed by the speed with which I transitioned from my man cave to the master bathroom, ripping off garments of clothing and leaving them in my wake. I was nearly naked by the time I arrived in the bathroom, hopping on one foot as I tore off my last sock. My underwear dangled from my ankle while I reached into the shower to turn on the water.

With blistering speed, I showered, shaved, and changed into my inconspicuous dinner attire. Getting into character for the evening's activities, I prepared myself for the mission ahead.

Tonight, our superhero/deployed contractor returns home after spending another three months on the battlefields of Afghanistan, dodging bullets while overseeing the construction of a top secret facility that will house the US arsenal's latest warfighting technology. Disguised as a mild-mannered baby boomer dressed in dinner slacks with loafers (no socks), a long-sleeved shirt rolled up to the forearms, matching belt, Omega Seamaster watch, and a pullover sweater tied around the shoulders, our contractor prepares himself for yet another challenging mission: rekindle his marriage by wining and dining his lovely wife with champagne and sumptuous cuisine.

I've always had a fertile imagination, but whenever I took leave I couldn't help but feel excited about being home, relaxing, and spending quality time with my wife. As I made my final preparations before heading downstairs, I clipped the clasp on my watch and looked at myself in the mirror. Absent from my reflection were the cargo pants and untucked shirt I usually wore. I didn't have a pistol, knife, or cell phone clipped to my belt. The ID badge dangling around my neck wasn't there, and I didn't miss it, not one single bit.

As I walked into the other room, to check on Barbara, I wasn't surprised to see that she hadn't made much progress. Barbara isn't fond of the fact that I can get dressed faster than she does, so she pretended not to notice me. Taking inventory of her status, I noted the situation as being NSTR: Nothing Significant To Report. She was still half-naked. Once I had lingered longer than I should have, she grew annoyed by my presence, dispensed with the ruse of pretending not to see me, and gave me my marching orders: "Go downstairs and watch TV," she huffed with exasperation.

"We're not going to the prom, Barb," I replied in jest. "How much longer is this going to take?" I wasn't really concerned over how long she needed, I was simply playing another set of verbal tennis and trying to score whatever points I could.

"Cinque minuti," she replied.

Cinque minuti (chink-way meen-ootee—Italian: five minutes) are two of Barbara's favorite words and her way of saying that she'll be ready in five minutes. I say that these are two of her favorite words because she repeats them constantly. Whenever she says these two words, I think, *Yeah, right.* Like all wives who make their husbands wait while they finish with whatever it is they're doing, i.e., brushing their hair, applying lipstick, taking something out of the freezer, etc., five minutes turns into a half hour.

Barbara says *cinque minuti* every time she needs another twenty minutes to complete whatever she's doing. According to Barbara's internal timekeeping mechanism, twenty minutes in the real world can be compressed into a time frame that feels like five minutes to her. In effect, whenever she says *cinque minuti*, I know I have at least fifteen minutes to play with, which was perfect, because now there was time to whip myself up a cocktail from my in-house, custom-made bar.

Whenever I told the story of my bar (and I did so with passion), my contractor cohorts became green with envy. Men are storytellers by nature, especially about things that are near and dear to their hearts. Some men tell tales of fishing and hunting expeditions, while others reminisce over the details of how they barbecued ribs at the family reunion, installed a new racing cam in their hot rod, or shot three birdies during their last round of golf. Like all good men, I'm a storyteller, too, and the one you're about to read touches on a subject that is dear to not only me, but the men I hung out with—the real men. This is the story of my bar.

I was home on leave. After spending ten days in Egypt, Barbara and I returned home to Bahrain. With three days still left before I needed to return to work, I was still feeling that relaxed mood; I hadn't yet begun to contemplate getting on that plane or regretting the fact that I'd be leaving home and returning to less-than-desirable living conditions—again.

On this particular day, Barbara and I were browsing through a local furniture store. One of the beauties of living in Arabia was that it offers an abundance of locally produced merchandise. There are handmade carpets and scores of interesting wall hangings and knick-knacks for the house. In Bahrain, we picked up bargain deals on custom-made jewelry, tailored clothing, and high-quality furnishings handmade by local craftsmen.

Barbara was looking at things for the house while I tagged along, perusing the aisles with no intention of buying anything. In the midst of what seemed like a sea of gaudy, ornate furnishings, I noticed a handcrafted bar. The exterior consisted of repeating geometric patterns, the likes of which covered the older-style Arabic windows. The wood was dark and deeply polished, giving the bar a rich and elegant appearance. I was so impressed, I sought out the proprietor of the shop and asked him the price. The shop merchant told me the unit had already been sold but explained that he could arrange to build another one just like it. The price: 250 Bahraini dinars, or approximately 660 US dollars.

I was intrigued. Even Barbara agreed that it was a fine piece of furniture, but she wasn't sold on the idea of having an actual bar in our home. I'll admit to feeling shamefully smitten, but I didn't want to hassle putting down a deposit and waiting for the finished product; I was headed back to work in a couple of days, and I had more important things to think about, like making the most of whatever time off I had left.

After returning to Afghanistan, I got to thinking about how much I admired that bar. The more I thought about it, the more I grew convinced I had to have it. Several months later, I returned home on R&R and sought out the shop merchant. Seeing he had a fish in the barrel, the clever merchant upped the price from 250 to 400 dinars. Claiming that he had too many other orders pending, he couldn't quote me the original price, and if I wanted the bar, I'd have to pay an additional fee. It was a good move, because he could see I wanted it, and I did.

"If I place the order today, when can you have the bar finished?" I asked.

"It'll take a couple of months," he replied. "I can't turn my back on all the other projects we've already started, and I won't compromise on the quality of this piece—if you're willing to spend the extra money."

I couldn't decide whether I hated this guy or respected the hell out of him. He was earning my business using techniques I applied on a routine basis.

"I'm leaving in three days, and I won't be back for three months," I reported to the merchant. "Is that enough time?"

"Absolutely," he said. "Don't worry about a thing. I'll deliver it to your house when I'm finished. It'll be waiting for you when you return."

"All right," I conceded. "Build it."

I didn't flinch when he asked for a 50 percent deposit, but when I told Barbara, she let out a gasp.

"Are you crazy?" she said. "You'll be lucky to ever see that thing. The deposit you just handed him was almost as much as the full price for the other bar."

I was aware of that, but I had given him the money in anticipation of eventually receiving what I'd set my sights on. Over the next three leave cycles, I visited the merchant in hopes of seeing a completed piece. Each time, however, he came up with a new excuse, and I grew furiously impatient. The only thing worse than being lied to was hearing Barbara's banter; she made a point of reminding me each month that the merchant had failed to deliver on his promise.

Eleven months after placing the deposit, the merchant finally delivered the handcrafted masterpiece to our home, and it was gorgeous. During the waiting period, I spent over $700 on marquee-labeled spirits to stock the shelves. My hope was to have some friends over and impress them with my new toy. My visions of grandeur were overshadowed by the fact that I didn't have any friends in Bahrain. I spent less than twenty days per year at home, and the rest of the time I was either in Afghanistan or on holiday somewhere with Barbara. Like many of the overzealous plans I had made in haste or out of touch with reality, this one too would require some modification.

Having dressed for dinner, I headed downstairs to the dining room, for a cocktail from my brand-new, well-stocked bar. Barbara had stated (again) that she needed *cinque minuti* to finish getting dressed, so this gave me plenty of time to pour myself a drink. As I came down the stairs, I realized I didn't need anyone to converse with over cocktails, so I did what came naturally: I sparked up a conversation with myself. That might sound a little strange, but I talked to myself all the

Photo from author's collection.

time while holed up in my hooch in Afghanistan. I talked to the TV, I spoke out loud practicing what I would say to customers, employees, or the corporate office, etc., so why change the program?

The following conversation actually took place between myself and The Other Me, whom I'll refer to as TOM.

TOM: "Wow, this is a *big* house. Nice place you have here, Kev."

Myself: "Thanks, buddy, but I don't live here, remember? It's my wife's place. I just visit from time to time—and pay the bills, of course."

TOM: "Can *I* marry you?" (I was quite impressed with myself.)

Myself: "Show me the ring and I'll think about it." I snorted.

TOM: "So...where's this bar you've been bragging about?"

Myself: "Right over here, my friend," I replied, motioning toward the bar. "Check this out!"

As I walked up to the bar, I stopped, made a sweeping motion with my arm, palm extended and gleaming with pride. Drew Carey couldn't have done a better job presenting the showcase prize on *The Price Is Right*.

Myself: "There she is, my pride, my joy." The look of satisfaction on my face was parallel to that of a father laying eyes upon his newborn son.

TOM: "Uh...bro? That doesn't even look like a bar. It's some sort of boxy-looking thing. What do you have in there, a TV?"

Myself: "Nope. But it does put on quite a show—observe."

I opened the cabinet doors, revealing the precious artifacts inside: neatly aligned bottles of bourbon, whiskey, scotch, vodka, rum, and an assortment of vintage wines were on display as if they were treasures in a museum. If there had been a harp in the room, we would have heard a flurry of chords. Had George Lucas directed this scene, he would have commissioned Industrial Light & Magic to create digital renderings of golden beams of light bursting from the interior of the bar. TOM and I would have to don sunglasses to protect our eyes from the intensity of light radiating from within the cabinet.

TOM: "I think I'm going to cry, man. That's beautiful." TOM was sniffing as if holding back tears.

Photo from author's collection.

Myself: "Isn't it, though?" I replied, as if beholding a miracle. "When I'm in Afghanistan, I cry myself to sleep just thinking about her."

My silly solo conversation was interrupted by Barbara yelling from the top of the stairs. "Who are you talking to...is someone here?"

"I'm just talking to myself, Barb," I hollered back. *Busted.*

"Aren't you ready yet? I added. *Sometimes it's better when you turn the tables. The best defense is a good offense.*

"Cinque minuti," she responded.

"Perfect," I replied under my breath.

The top of the scotch bottle I had selected was corked and had to be twisted off to be removed. It made that classic popping sound as I pulled it free from the neck of the bottle. *Beautiful.* I poured two fingers of the dark amber liquid into a crystal tumbler and held the glass above my head in front of the chandelier. I was mesmerized by all the different colors of light being refracted through the glass and the liquid inside. Next, I took a slow but healthy swig and felt the warmth of the scotch slipping down my throat into my chest. The sensation was strong but not overwhelming, and the effect of the alcohol absorbing into the soft tissue of my core was immediate. I was buzzed.

After exhaling slowly, I took inventory of my senses and all that lay before me. Our 1,200-square-foot living room was adorned with new furnishings on three eight-by-twelve-foot Persian rugs. The dining room table had never hosted a party, but it was paid for, like everything else we owned. The wall hangings, marble floors, swimming pool—all of it was testament to a level of success I had never anticipated but felt pride for having achieved. At that moment, I realized I was as far from Afghanistan as I needed to be. I was at home among the trophies of my success.

While absorbed in my thoughts, I began to consider all that had been created from the insanity of a world that had drawn me to where I stood. I had gained so much, but it had come at a high price: in exchange for my good fortune, I had lost both time and fragments of my former self. It was a lot to absorb, so I shifted focus back onto the item responsible for my latest distraction: my bar. Between the rich fragrance of its rosewood composition and another healthy draw from the crystal glass in my hand, nothing else seemed to matter at that moment; I was home, and I would enjoy what little time I had left. Soon it would be time for me to go back to work—back to the place where uncertainty loomed and my destiny awaited.

CHAPTER ELEVEN

The End Game

As a civilian contractor, I was afforded the opportunity to experience Afghanistan from a variety of perspectives. I worked on numerous military bases, supporting literally dozens of projects worth hundreds of millions of dollars. I traveled throughout the country on airplanes, helicopters, and up-armored and soft vehicles. During this rather unique period of my life, I was well paid, accomplished a great deal in terms of professional and personal growth, and had one hell of good time—most of the time, at least.

Looking back, I always felt most comfortable while I was employed by the Turks. They were some of the most skilled, professional, and kindest people I worked with during my tenure as a contractor in Afghanistan. The trust they placed in me was humbling, and I guarded their faith with great care. Occasionally, I was required to attend meetings at the home front office in Ankara, Turkey. Whenever Barbara accompanied me, they extended every courtesy imaginable. They sent a driver in the company sedan to pick us up at the airport and booked us at the finest hotels. While I attended business meetings, Barbara was given a private tour of the city and taken shopping by one of the secretaries. The evenings would include a gala dinner attended by company executives, who stood in line to meet us as we entered the restaurant. I'd shake hands with familiar colleagues, who in turn offered quick salutations before shifting their attention to Barbara. In keeping with Italian protocol, Barbara would kiss each of the men twice, once on each cheek (right side first) and they would glow with pride, as would I.

"Don't mind me, fellas, I'll be at the bar while you all kiss my wife," I joked.

"That's a good idea, Kevin," mused my boss, the vice president of operations. His right hand was holding one of Barbara's hands while his left hand was shooing me away in jest. "We see enough of you as it is, go on!"

Everyone laughed and smiled in their business attire: coats, ties, and evening dresses. The smell of cologne and the sound of ice cubes tinkling in cocktail glasses was a welcome change. *Beats the hell out of being in Afghanistan.*

The experience I had while working with the Turks was productive, profitable, and most of all, pleasant. Like all good things, nothing lasts forever and my tenure with the Turks was destined to run its course. I knew that we'd have to part company, one day, but I was hoping to postpone it for as long as possible.

The ending didn't come suddenly. It took several months, and came in the form of another opportunity I was reluctant to consider: a handsome offer from an American firm supporting military construction projects throughout Afghanistan. Eventually, I succumbed to the notion that the time for me to move on was approaching, and the opportunity presented to me was a good one, or so it seemed.

The job change conundrum I wrestled with reminded me of a time while I was serving in the Navy. I was working as a military instructor and doing some collateral work as a part-time journalist producing a newsletter for the battalion. My literary skills were noticed by a senior officer from our parent command at the regiment, a gentleman who happened to be the former executive officer (XO) from our battalion. While I was sitting in my office, going over some lesson plans, the XO dropped by and told me about a vacancy within the regiment's public affairs office. He said I'd be perfect for the job and encouraged me to come aboard. What I didn't know at the time was that the XO hadn't notified my superiors of his intention to speak with me, and according to military protocol, that's a pretty big no-no.

The prospect of leaving the battalion and working for our parent command was equivalent to being given a promotion. I enjoyed the work I was doing as an instructor, but serving as a full-time journalist appealed to me as well; military journalists are given access to every corner of the armed forces. Having a chance to see and learn more about the Navy interested me. Changing jobs, however, was a tough decision, and I didn't know how to approach the opportunity without ruffling a few feathers.

Adding further complication to the mix, when my commanding officer (CO) found out the XO was sidelining as a headhunter, he gave him an ass-chewing that was heard throughout battalion headquarters. Afterward, the CO called me into this office and lectured me on loyalty and the importance of supporting our unit within my current assignment. I hadn't done a thing beyond listening to the XO's sales pitch. I hadn't given any indication as to whether or not I was even considering the offer, and yet I'd been called on the carpet and made to feel like a traitor.

At the end of a rather stern lecture, the CO gave me some time to think over my decision, but his preference was clear: he didn't want me leaving the unit. In retrospect, I don't think it had anything to do with needing me; he simply wasn't about to release me after being outflanked by a fellow officer who had dared to enter his kingdom without announcing his presence or intention.

Shaken, intimidated, and confused, I shared what had happened with a lieutenant commander with whom I had served for several years.

"Let me tell you something, Kevin," he said (and I'll never forget his words). "Opportunities present themselves when things are going well."

"What would you do, Commander?" I asked. "I don't want to piss off the Skipper, and yet the chance to work at the regiment—doing something I'm really good at—that sounds pretty exciting."

"You're the only who can make that decision," the Lieutenant Commander replied. "My advice is to trust your instincts and don't worry about what other people think."

When I informed the CO that I wanted to transfer to the regiment, he was cooperative with my decision yet displeased. It wasn't as if I had decided to leave the Rebellion and fight for the Evil Empire, but he still wasn't happy. Fortunately, my decision turned out to be a good one. I was given the opportunity to do everything I had hoped for and more. I traveled throughout the US, writing stories and providing photos for Navy periodicals published around the world. I participated in the Navy's July 4th millennium celebration in New York City and attended a media event at the top of the World Trade Center. During that assignment, I met a Navy journalist who encouraged me to apply for a position as a temporary journalist aboard an aircraft carrier slotted for a six-month Western Pacific (WESTPAC) deployment. I subsequently applied for the position, was accepted, and fulfilled a boyhood dream: I sailed aboard an aircraft carrier, the USS Constellation (CV-64), "America's Flagship." I launched off the flight deck aboard an S-3 Viking, served on reconnaissance and refueling missions, and trapped in the arresting wires aboard the carrier—six times. While sailing the deep blue sea as a proud member of the US Navy, I realized I had accomplished several of my lifelong goals by remaining true to what my father had told me: "You can do anything you want in life, son...all you have to do is want it bad enough, and eventually you'll accomplish whatever you set your sights upon." My dad was right. *Thanks, Dad.*

The job the Americans offered me provided an opportunity for me to test my skills further: I would be tasked with overseeing and directing project managers who were supervising the execution of multiple contracts worth hundreds of millions of dollars. The American firm who approached me was of considerable clout and experience. They were less capable than the Turks in terms of being able to self-perform their work, but they had an advantage over the Turks: they were vetted and preapproved by the US government as one of several companies who could compete and bid on Heavy Engineering Repair and Construction (HERC) contracts. The HERC contracts represented a sizable slice of the US-funded projects in Afghanistan. If you were a building contractor (like me), HERC contracts offered attractive opportunities for continuous work.

Prior to my employment with the Americans, the same company had approached the Turks for support on a new contract they had landed in Shindand. Connecting with a HERC contractor appealed to the Turks: more business equaled greater profits. During a joint meeting between our two companies, the CEO of the American firm took me aside and expressed an interest in hiring me. I was flattered by the gesture, but politely turned him down, explaining that my loyalty was to my current employers, who had hired me to expand their business interests—which included doing business with *his* company.

Four months later, the American firm found itself in a delightful pickle; the US government had awarded them over $800 million in new contracts (all at once), and they were determined to find qualified help to assist them in executing the huge volume of work. I was asked again to come aboard, but I politely refused, saying I had a good thing going with the Turks and that I wasn't ready to part company. In an effort to help my company's business partners, I offered the services of a colleague who worked with Kurt, the retired Army colonel I mentioned earlier. Getting a better job with a higher-paying salary enabled my colleague to advance his career and earn more money—a lot more money, in fact.

During a meeting with their new employee (my colleague), one of the program managers for the American firm took me aside and told me that they had a key position that his company needed to fill: "We want you to come and work for us, Kevin," he said. "We need another program manager, and we want you for the job."

"Dammit!" I replied. I didn't want to spoil my relationship with the Turks. I was intrigued, however, by the prospect of taking on more responsibility—and earning more money.

"Let me put you in touch with our VP of construction," the program manager said. "I know he'll make you a good offer, and you can decide if it's right for you."

Before the negotiations had begun, I felt I had nothing to lose, so I bargained hard. In the end, the Americans agreed to a monthly salary that penciled out to about $300,000 per year. It was a lot of money and a tough decision; I didn't want to leave the Turks, but the writing was on the wall: President Obama had promised to fix the US economy *and* end the war in Afghanistan. Accomplishing both objectives would require a cessation of funding for the type of projects I had been supporting for the past seven years. The question, therefore, was no longer a matter of *if* the jobs downrange would dry up, but *when*.

I spoke with Barbara and explained the complexities of the decision. It was lot for both of us to absorb, because of the emotional attachment we had made; the Turks had treated us with overwhelming kindness and generosity. To arrive at a decision I'd be comfortable with, I needed to discuss my situation with my boss, the VP of operations with the Turkish company. I never told him what the Americans had offered me because I would never disrespect him by implying I would use it as leverage. Fortunately, he was (and still is) an astute businessman who could compartmentalize life's components into their proper contexts without getting emotional. After a series of phone calls and consultations with his colleagues, my boss advised me to take the job with the Americans, with one caveat: continue trying to expand both companies' mutual interests. It was a fair plan that would enable everyone to part company as friends.

The data points I used in making my decision included bankrolling some funds we'd need to restore our home in Italy. Barbara had inherited a seventy-year-old house in Tuscany from her late uncle, and the place needed a complete overhaul. The price for restoring a house in Italy is about three times what it costs in America, so for the first time in my experience as a forward-deployed contractor, money played a role in my decision-making. Nothing in life comes with a guarantee, but I calculated that if I could last just one year with the Americans, then I could put away an even heftier sum of money than I had accrued thus far. Moreover, if I was fortunate enough to leave Afghanistan before getting hurt (or killed), I could accomplish both my personal and financial goals: testing my professional ability at another level, and bankrolling an even larger sum of money. Once again, therefore, I took another leap of faith. With fingers crossed, I counted on the success I'd had in the past. Unbeknownst to me, at the time, was the fact that my luck, or good fortune, was about to change.

Within a few days of changing jobs, my hopes for a positive future were dashed. I had traded the comfort and security of the Turkish compound for a rented frat house in Wazir Akbar Khan, an upscale residential area of Kabul that resembled a high-end ghetto. My private living quarters consisted of a large bedroom and a shared bathroom within a ten-bedroom super villa. With offices in the basement, we lived and worked on the same premises, twenty-four hours a day.

Photo from author's collection.

The location of the villa, and the furnishings and decor, left much to be desired, at least from my point of view, but I'd been spoiled; working for the Turks was equivalent to life membership at a country club. Serving as business development manager for the Turks was like being a member of the royal family.

The American company's villa was on a dirt road about a mile from Kabul's green zone. The potholes in the street were deep and capable of damaging the front end of even the sturdiest four by four. Mangy dogs and feral cats were everywhere. Barbed wire was placed atop the sixteen-foot walls that protected our villa, but a serious intruder could have breached our perimeter with little difficulty. A steel gate served as the entrance to a parking lot that housed four vehicles and within the compound worked a small detachment of Afghan security guards armed (only) with hand-held radios. As I laid eyes upon our pathetic quick reaction force, I could imagine my fate...

(Static) *"Ahmet to Mohammed, do you read me?"*

(Beeping sound) *"Go ahead Ahmet, what is it?"*

(Static) *"...the Taliban are here, demanding we turn over the Americans...what should I do?"*

(Beep) *"Let them in the gate, habibi—and run!"*

My new digs featured a leaky roof, stained walls, mismatched furniture, dirty carpets, broken floor tiles, and dingy drapes. Reality TV's home improvement celebs Scott and Amie Yancey from *Flipping Vegas* would have landed in divorce court over this project. It was ugly!

No one else at our villa seemed to complain about our living arrangements, which led me to believe that my colleagues were either accustomed to living in similar (or worse) conditions, or ignored the seediness of their surroundings given the high salaries they were being paid. The company had made a great effort to capture the finest crop of builders they could acquire, and the salaries they paid were substantially higher than what other companies were willing to offer.

Most of the men I worked with didn't share my desire for living in comfort. A toilet, shower, and a cocktail lounge down the street seemed to satisfy most of their requirements. The front office (back in the US) was aware that employees were carousing in the lounges outside the wire after hours, but they turned a blind eye. One of the biggest partyers within our villa complex was the security manager, who was a nice guy, actually. Everyone liked him, but he wasn't what I'd call a poster child for personal protection; he showed up for work one morning with a black eye and bum leg. Eyewitnesses to the previous evening's escapades snickered while telling a story of how he'd tripped and fallen on his face while attempting to walk home after a night of heavy drinking.

As I settled into my surroundings, I noticed that many of our project engineers and quality control (QC) personnel were Afghan locals, Indians, and Pakistanis—young, third country nationals (TCNs) who were in their late twenties and early thirties. Every project required certified QCs to meet the US government's contract requirements, but whenever local hires were incorporated into projects costing upwards of $10 million, it got my antennae buzzing. The younger TCN engineers rarely had much field experience, and the average Afghan builder didn't know the first thing about US building standards. In either case, the engineers may have come equipped with the certifications and degrees that our contracts stipulated, but whether they could even read a set of drawings (in English) or measure up to the US government's high expectations was another matter entirely.

Adding yet another challenge was the fact that most of the TCNs were intimidated by our clients, whose ranks were frequently populated by hard-nosed US government (USG) employee bureaucrats who took pleasure in holding a contractor's feet to the fire.

Hiring TCN engineers on the cheap saved the company money, but it cost our company in other areas that would come back to haunt them. Most of our foreign engineering staff had never worked on projects even remotely similar to the multimillion-dollar contracts we'd been awarded. They weren't prepared for the pressure they'd be under from government agents with high expectations and little tolerance for even the most minute miscalculation.

The complexities of the USG's contracting mechanism posed challenges for even the most prolific builders. Agreeing to embark on projects worth tens of millions of dollars, was extremely risky. The profit margins were slim. Projects developed to US standards were often impossible to build anywhere but in America, and the challenges associated with creating workaround solutions were routinely nightmarish and prohibitively counterproductive. Stringent building standards and rigid timelines quickly overwhelmed the inexperienced local hires and TCNs. Very few of our foreign engineers and QCs could keep up with their workloads—let alone comprehend the weight of the responsibility they'd been given. Making matters worse, most of the local design firms we had secured were no better. Technical drawings and design submittals were so poor that they were repeatedly rejected for failing to follow written instructions.

On construction projects, technical designs must be approved before any work begins. Consequently, before many of our projects had broken ground, they were already behind schedule. When our senior management (back in the US) became aware of these repeated delays, their reaction was to deploy alternative, low-cost solutions. In other words, one ineffective design firm was exchanged for another. Between our inexperienced local staff and the ill-equipped local design firms—who failed to possess the working knowledge that could satisfy the USG plan checkers—there was a high turnover rate among those who were bought on the cheap to accommodate the company's low-bidder/job-getter strategy.

As I studied the material estimates for my projects, I noticed the company had overlooked some important details that should have been incorporated into our construction budgets, details that were overlooked during the bid review. Concerned, I set out to determine how so many errors could have been made. After consulting with several colleagues, I learned that many of our contract-winning proposals had used estimates submitted by local national (LN, Afghan) subcontractors. Through the provision of an attractive low-ball bid, the Afghan subs were hoping to earn our business once the contract was awarded. Unfortunately, their strategy worked, and problems ensued.

Using outside sources to assist in developing proposals is a common practice throughout the construction industry; prime contractors solicit cost estimates from subcontractors all the time. The extent to which these takeoffs (material cost and labor calculation/ estimates) are used, however, can get a company in trouble. As I dug deeper, I discovered examples of where the company was hasty in submitting its bids to the government. One of our new contracts used a local contractor's bid that neglected to include several million dollars of heating and air-conditioning equipment for an aircraft hangar. Another bid had neglected to include money for security forces to protect a jobsite located in Taliban territory.

Case after case revealed missing materials and insufficient labor calculations. Over-burdened by a huge backlog of projects, and in keeping with their policy of awarding contracts to the lowest compliant bidder, the US government had failed to identify numerous deficiencies in our bid that would lead to construction delays, resulting in follow-on discussions of additional funding. That such errors were committed by design seems unlikely, but such oversights were advantageous. My company could argue that they needed more time to recover from delays incurred by others—including those who awarded the contract. At ground level, my project managers and I had doubts that the outcome of our findings would yield anything but calamity. We seriously doubted that our projects could be completed using what little money had been allocated for such lofty and expensive endeavors. The company had rolled the dice and was gambling with some very high stakes.

Ten out of ten business moguls will agree that *growth* is one of the factors that kills most successful enterprises. Modern scholars have theorized that the collapse of the Mayan civilization was in part due both to political upheaval, and environmental degradation; the Mayan population consumed its surrounding natural resources faster than they could be replenished. The Roman Empire faced similar problems with political corruption, but the empire's biggest problem lay in the fact that its territory was simply too vast to control. The conquest of the Roman Empire lasted from 31 BC to 476 AD. Afterward, Rome's conquered countries resumed their former existences (plus or minus whatever improvements had been accrued), and the glory of Rome became a memory for historians and tourists to ponder.

Successful companies hoping to expand are often met with total failure when growth plans either don't exist, are poorly engineered, or aren't followed. After a fairly successful campaign through Russia, the German army could see the spires of the Kremlin in Moscow before being hit by a blizzard that stopped them in their tracks. Ill-prepared for the Russian winter, the Germans froze, starved, and were pummeled by their climatically adept adversaries. Operation Barbarossa (the Axis invasion of the Soviet Union) cost the German army 830,000 men and was the prelude to an unconditional surrender that ended the European campaign against Nazi Germany.

At the American firm where I worked, things were unraveling all over Afghanistan, and in retrospect, all the signs were blinking like warning lights. With several dozen projects running simultaneously, the overhead expenses were staggering. Meanwhile, many of the Afghan companies we hired as subcontractors were failing to perform, and the impact was creating a ripple effect throughout the company. Without being able to submit invoices for progress payments, which had been calculated and were counted on every month to sustain the company's huge overhead, the company's ambitious growth plan mirrored White Star Line's launching of the RMS *Titanic* from Southampton to New York. The prominent and successful British shipping company hoped to obtain a record-breaking Atlantic crossing and worldwide fame. Ignoring risk, the ship's captain set a course through a known ice field, sealing the "unsinkable" vessel's fate.

I found parallels between the fate of the *Titanic* and my American employers, who, like White Star Line (and their impetuous captain) had known great success before biting off more than they could chew. Before I describe the carnage that occurred, let me continue with the story of our voyage; everyone loves a good tragedy.

Most of the projects downrange were suffering from the same problem: poor execution. Having a crackerjack team of American construction managers failed to influence the results of having an Afghan workforce that was unmoved by the American firm's need for progress. As the noose began to tighten, so, too, did the stress levels, especially at higher headquarters, back in the US. One of our senior field managers was fired for challenging an aggressive and overbearing US government contracting officer, for impeding an Afghan subcontractor from executing work. Eventually, the Afghans grew frustrated and stopped trying. When the project hit a standstill, our CEO fired the field manager for failure to exercise diplomacy with our belligerent client. He should have given the field manager a pay raise for his efforts at trying to protect the company's interests, but instead he canned him. *Whiskey, Tango, Foxtrot.*

Shortly thereafter, several project managers came to me expressing concerns over the condition of the company. They weren't paranoid, they were perceptive—dead-on, in fact. Most of the PMs within my program were savvy builders who'd lived through the collapse of their own empires. They could see the endgame in sight. The world as they knew it was collapsing in front of them, and no one wanted to get hit by the falling debris.

My weekly work routine switched from visiting jobsites and checking on progress, to participating in teleconferences and face-to-face meetings with unhappy clients. The company CEO was losing his cool during telecoms between the US and our field operations. He could see the gravity of the crisis growing as the percentage of billable work continued to slide. Everyone in the field could sense that he was under a great deal of pressure, but few were willing to overlook his condescending tone or the expectation for field operations to remedy what the front office had created: a recipe for disaster.

Most of our contracts were bid with only enough money to hire local firms, who were untested at the levels we needed them to perform.
Having worked in government contracting for many years, I understood the problems we were facing. Some of the issues were resolv-
able, while others would require collaboration with the US government, in ways that neither Uncle Sam nor my company would agree
on. As the situation worsened, the company faced a no-win scenario;
they appeared to hope for a miracle that would not occur.

No one was willing to admit what everyone could see but was
afraid to say. "The king isn't wearing any clothes"; the magic fabric
purchased by the king was nothing more than a sham. The corporate offices in the US had made promises to investors that fell short
of everyone's expectations. Disaster was imminent, but fear prevented people from facing reality before lofty strategies proved totally
ineffective.

Downrange, my project managers were having little success per-
suading their less-than-motivated Afghan subcontractors to stay focused—let alone show up for work. During a contract termination
conference with one of our more problematic subs, the country manager and I had the duty of informing a local outfit that they were being terminated for failure to execute their contract on time. Losing a
contract was bad enough, but after losing face and being dishonored,
the Afghan subcontractor filed a lawsuit. To our astonishment and
dismay (and in accordance with Afghan law), the Afghan police were
dispatched to pick up the defendants of the lawsuit (the country manager and I), who were to be taken to jail while awaiting a settlement
hearing. The country manager and I were befuddled yet concerned
for our well-being. The Taliban had been terrorizing the country for
decades, but the local constable was hell-bent on putting us in jail
over a civil matter that wouldn't survive five minutes in Judge Judy's
courtroom.

You can't make this stuff up, I thought to myself. *And I thought my
bad luck for abandoning the cat was behind me.*

Spending time behind bars in an Afghan prison wasn't stipulated in my contract, so I hightailed it across the desert to another project site on a US military installation—inside the wire. In the cargo hold of my SUV were my luggage and a pair of Gorilla boxes. Gorilla boxes were black plastic, elongated storage containers for stowing all the extra stuff people acquired in theater. Next to all the white Toyota SUVs and black Chevy Suburbans that were sold, Gorilla boxes were probably one of the most popular items purchased, but that's another story.

Back on the project site (where the subcontractor was terminated for cause), the owner of the Afghan company reported to his unpaid employees that the Americans had cheated them. When the workers heard this, they amassed at the entrance to the jobsite with a vengeance. The mob was met at the gates by our local (armed) Afghan security forces, but none of the guards were willing to risk their lives or gun down an angry citizen over a labor dispute. As the situation escalated, a detachment of US soldiers stationed nearby was contacted for assistance. Surprisingly, they refused to intervene, saying it wasn't their fight. Fortunately, and just before the angry locals stormed our jobsite, the company chartered a helicopter and airlifted our employees to safety.

My colleagues and I found it despicable that US forces wouldn't come to the aid of US citizens in jeopardy. We saw it as treason and a testament to the fact that America had already conceded defeat: we had lost the war in Afghanistan and no one seemed to care. Sadder still was the fact that such stories never made the news.

The cost of the war in Afghanistan had exceeded everyone's expectations. Sweeping reductions were made to mitigate the effects of what would be an expensive demobilization. Removing itself from the grip of decade-long war that cost nearly a trillion US dollars included budget cuts that were shameful, if not unlawful. The US government stopped providing meal service for many of the US expats who dined at the DFAC. Next, they restricted access to the US postal service. In some cases, US civilian contractors were told they wouldn't receive a

CAC ID card, which in effect denied them access to the US military bases where they were supposed to be working. As the government struggled to figure out its exit strategy, the bureaucracy was running amok, and even the warfighters were asking my favorite question: *WTF?*

Similar instances of chaos were occurring on jobsites throughout the country. Blu, the affable and energetic colleague from Utah, was serving on a project where he and several members of his staff had to sneak out of their contractor camp in the middle of the night to avoid being captured by an angry mob of unpaid Afghan workers. I was disappointed to learn that Blu was also denied support from a detachment of US forces near his project. Blu later confided he had never felt so scared and betrayed. He was lucky to come away from the incident with nothing more than a story that surpassed our rocket attack on Christmas.

As the number and intensity of problems with our business in Afghanistan increased, the outcome seemed inevitable: many of our projects couldn't be completed, and the government would be forced to examine alternative solutions, such as terminating our contracts, retendering them for bid by others, or abandoning them altogether. My suggestion was to recommend to the USG that they terminate some our projects for convenience. A number of projects were being hindered as a result of being subjected to attacks in hostile areas; we couldn't bring in materials, and in some cases the labor force was too afraid to come to work; they didn't want to be killed on the highway while commuting to the jobsite.

I knew that whenever a project had been terminated at the government's convenience, the contractor of record was held harmless and released without penalty. Without even a moment of consideration, however, my suggestion was dismissed.

"We're not going to ask the government to terminate any of our projects," barked the vice president of operations.

The VP's response was telling yet disappointing. Refusing to request any form of contractual sanctuary suggested to me that the company was either in denial over the gravity of our circumstances, or hoping to maintain a ruse for its investors. Eventually, even the VP had to go on the lam; the Afghan police forces came looking for him, too. At one point in time, there were about six of us dodging the local law, but we took it in stride. We joked about being among the privileged few who were actually wanted by the Afghans.

Upon hearing the VP's directive to stand firm, one of my project managers (who was overseeing a financially challenged project within a hostile territory) resigned. He wasn't about to risk his life in support of a lost cause. Six months later, that same project was terminated by the government for default. Like the subcontractor we had terminated for nonperformance, the US government cut ties with our company for similar reasons: we weren't producing.

Continuing to work with the local, lowball firms who were unable to meet time-sensitive deadlines was a death sentence. In desperation, the company tried to self-perform the work, rather than rely on others who lacked the skills and motivation to succeed. Self-performing the work was a good idea, but it would require manpower and equipment our delinquent subcontractors had failed to provide. It was a workable solution, but the capital needed to frontload these activities either hadn't been considered, or wasn't available. After analyzing the cost to self-perform the projects within my $300 million program, I submitted a report to our corporate headquarters that outlined a need for $30 million in cash within the next three months. Without this money, the projects I was responsible for would fall further behind schedule and eventually fail.

My report to corporate headquarters was either poorly received or a wakeup call that led to my own demise. In the wake of numerous employee dismissals, aimed at reducing our overhead—as well as several voluntary departures from people who didn't want to go down with the ship—I knew I was on borrowed time. In due course, my destiny would match that of the Roman couriers who were ordered to be executed by the emperor for bringing him bad news. On the one-year anniversary of my hire date with the American company, I was terminated. Thirty minutes earlier, I was having breakfast with the project manager whom I had helped secure employment a year earlier. We were talking about the deterioration of the company, and he expressed concerns over losing his job.

"Don't worry," I told him. "They're not going to fire you—they're going to fire me. I'm one of the highest-paid field employees that hasn't been let go. The company is bleeding cash. I'm next; you'll see."

I hate it when I'm right. With the foresight of Nostradamus, I had predetermined my own fate. If there was any consolation, it was that I had survived exactly one year. Sustaining employment for one year enabled me to accomplish my financial objective. I would have liked to stay longer, but it didn't work out that way. My fate was determined once I decided to jump ship with the Turks for a chance at more money and responsibility.

Commensurate with the company's indifferent approach toward maintaining minimum morale standards, my employers gave me twenty-four hours to pack my bags and be on a plane bound for home. Per my "at will" contract, no explanation for my dismissal was required, so none was offered. The country manager (someone I'd developed a cordial relationship with) had the unfortunate task of letting me go. At the end of our short, five-minute termination conference, we shook hands and he left me alone to contemplate the end of my seven-year career as war zone contractor.

Being terminated felt strange, for not since the eleventh grade had I been fired from a job. The first time I got fired, I was working as a night janitor at the Automobile Club of America in Van Nuys, California. My coworkers and I were goofing around one night, and we neglected to clean the conference room. Apparently, that was a damnable offense, because all three of us got canned the next day.

The end of the company's tenure in Afghanistan was a bloodbath. Six months after my termination, the country manager either resigned or was forced out by a new corporate management team, whose mission was to collect whatever scraps of value could be retained from among the carnage. Sometime thereafter, the vice president (who, in my RMS *Titanic* analogy, was responsible for the ship's propulsion) was either thrown overboard by White Star Line's new executives or elected to jump ship before the stern disappeared beneath the waves. The unsympathetic company CEO lost his job, and the president of the company, who owned a financial interest in the failing contracts, was rendered powerless.

Ironically (or perhaps by design), the guy at breakfast who was worried about losing his job was given my position. To his credit, he possessed the survival skills necessary to earn the admiration of the new management team.

For nearly a year after I left Afghanistan, many of my former colleagues were still employed while the US government terminated my former employer's remaining contracts, retendered whatever could be salvaged, or abandoning them entirely. During a telephone conversation with my replacement, he boasted of receiving a six-figure bonus for keeping the company's operations afloat just long enough for them to file Chapter Seven. I've always wondered if he remembered to include that bullet point on his résumé, but I digress—and no, I wasn't jealous of what he received—but I did feel rather stupid for overestimating his integrity as long as I did.

I felt torn by the notion that my career in Afghanistan had ended under such abysmal circumstances. I missed the routine; I wasn't prepared for such a radical change. I went from being engaged in doing something meaningful each day to doing nothing and feeling empty. What happened seemed unfair, but I realized that fairness had nothing to do with it. Fairness doesn't exist in war. There are those who survive, and those who don't.

A month after I was released from my contract, Barbara and I relocated from Bahrain to our home in Italy. Despite the appearance of feeling satisfied with my new circumstances, I wasn't. I had transitioned from being responsible for hundreds of millions of dollars in US government contracts to pushing the shopping cart for Barbara at the supermarket. I should have felt satisfied for having survived such a lengthy and challenging ordeal—without so much as a scratch—but I wasn't. I missed the excitement and the gratification that came with supporting what I had once believed was a noble cause.

CHAPTER TWELVE

Post Afghanistan

Our return to Italy seemed to mirror the mood that Barbara and I were in: sad, depressed, and discouraged. Neither one of us was keen on moving from our comfortable digs in Bahrain—not that there's anything wrong with relocating to Tuscany—it's a beautiful region. Beyond its picturesque landscapes and sumptuous cuisine, however, life for the average Tuscan is far different than what most tourists ever see. The cost of living in Italy's most popular region is high, yet life is still fairly simple. Owning a clothes dryer (for example) is considered a luxury. There's a certain charm associated with living a simpler life. I've found that people who live with less, are also less demanding, and oftentimes more pleasant.

During its warm five-month season, Forte Dei Marmi becomes a weekend/summer retreat for tourists, and well-to-do Italians who can afford a vacation home. The part-time residents consist mostly of city dwellers from Florence and Milan. In exchange for the seasonal revenue they provide, the oftentimes snobby Florentines and snooty Milanese are politely tolerated by the locals. British expats and affluent Russians have also purchased summer homes in Forte Dei Marmi, as well as a number of Italian celebrities. Magnificent yachts anchor off the coast so their posh passengers can spend an afternoon shopping at the local Gucci and Prada outlets, or spend an evening at one of

Forte Dei Marmi's iconic dining establishments: Ristorante Lorenzo, La Barca, Bistrot, and Osteria Del Marmi compose the short list of places to be seen.

During the off season, things quiet down considerably. Having arrived in the fall, when season was over, and the hordes of tourists and part-time residents had returned home, our abandoned beach town seemed appropriately melancholy.

Determined to reestablish some semblance of a normal life, I made routine trips to the pier to investigate how the local fishermen were doing. I never saw anything too impressive, but the old men were always out there, trying to catch something for dinner—and a story to go with it. Surfers in wetsuits sat patiently on their boards, hoping to catch a decent wave, but from my Southern California point of view there weren't any. The smell of the salt air and the view of the Italian coastline were relaxing, but it felt as though something was missing from my life. I didn't feel whole.

Beneath the facade of what appeared to be an aloof (or perhaps retired) American resident was an outcast civilian contractor from Afghanistan, struggling to understand what he had done wrong. I was far less comfortable than I tried to appear. The pace of my new lifestyle was far slower than what I had been accustomed to. I didn't have to wake up in the morning, so I didn't set the alarm clock. Barbara was up and about each morning; she wasn't about to lie around and feel sorry for her change in scenery—and she felt worse than I did about moving back home. Barbara is a fighter, a stubborn Tuscan who spared no time for moping around or feeling miserable; she had house chores to do, and a positive mind-set to maintain, which, to her credit, she accomplished with little distraction.

I didn't fare as well. I admit it. I felt as if I had been traveling aboard a high-speed train for the past ten years when suddenly, there I was, sitting in the middle of the tracks while the train sped away. The ride was over.

During my period of good fortune, I had accrued a sizable war chest that provided me the flexibility and financial independence I had worked to establish. My savings would allow me to remain comfortably unemployed for several years and enjoy the luxury of being selective with my next field of endeavor. However convenient that may sound, I knew that boredom would play a role in getting me back on my feet before long. That having been said, I was also looking forward to doing absolutely nothing, at least for a little while. Barbara stayed busy with her domestic chores: going to the supermarket and checking with the commune on the status of our home improvement project—which had taken a turn for the worse. Shortly after moving back to Italy, we learned that the approval process on our home renovation project would be delayed for six months. The news didn't sit well with me. In terms of construction projects ours was a cookie-cutter, at least by US standards; the approval process shouldn't have taken more than a month or two. I didn't know it at the time, but this was the first of many lessons I would learn about Italian bureaucracy. I wasn't in Kansas anymore.

With nothing on my calendar, I embraced even the most mundane of activities each day: I went to the post office to pay the bills, picked up the dry cleaning, and walked to the local hardware store to buy odds and ends for the house. I walked everywhere. Everything I needed to do was within walking distance. Having been raised in Los Angeles (where you drive everywhere and fight traffic), the small-town atmosphere of Forte Dei Marmi was a refreshing change. I tried to convince myself that the absence of concrete T-walls, barbed-wire fences with motion sensors, plywood B-Huts, and potato-sized river rock beneath my feet were yet another benefit, but oddly enough I missed all of that, too. I couldn't get Afghanistan out of my head.

I missed the routine of getting up every morning and knowing I was responsible for showing progress with my employer and our client. I felt pride in being associated with an activity that supported such a noble and badass objective as killing the zealots who supported the murder of US citizens on American soil. My colleagues and I were literally at the tip of the spear in terms of adding value to the military's warfighting machine, and with that effort came great pride. We were productive, arrogant, and justly confident. I knew that my time in Afghanistan wouldn't last forever, and that one day I'd be asked to step down and take a well-deserved rest. That decision hadn't been mine, however, and as a result I felt cheated. I pretended to feel good about my new surroundings, but I don't think I was fooling many people, except maybe myself.

Given all of the free time we had at our disposal, Barbara and I decided to stay in shape by taking a long walk after lunch every day. Describing it as a long walk would be an understatement, for in the words of my buddy Blu, "Man, it was a good one!" We walked fifteen kilometers (nine miles) every day, six days a week. Six months later, we were still walking, so I punched some numbers into the calculator and discovered that we had walked a distance that was greater than the length of the Italian peninsula. Even though we were walking (versus running), I think Forrest Gump would have been impressed.

Beyond all the cardio and aerobic benefits, the walking provided us time to talk about the future and figure out what we wanted to do next. However romantic and therapeutic that might sound, often we walked together without saying a word. I regret having to admit that there were too many times when a seemingly cordial conversation was disrupted by a disagreement that was usually prompted by me. I was suffering from what might best be described as *Bagram on the Brain,* or an acute case of *KAIA-phobia.* In layman's terms, you could say that my head was stuck in the past. I'd been forced to resign from a world where most everything was dictated by me. Hundreds of men had been under my care, custody, and control. I decided everything, from when I ate lunch to what time I hopped into my Toyota Land Cruiser and headed through the badlands—alone.

Everything in my post-Afghanistan world had changed. I was frustrated by the fact that I didn't have anything to do, with the exception of taking a long walk every day. As my frustration mounted, I resented the notion that our afternoon walks had transitioned into a mandatory, daily requirement.

"Hey, Barbara, how about we skip the walk and go out to lunch today?" I'd ask enthusiastically.

"We can't. We have to go on our walk." She was practical as ever, checking her watch to ensure we wouldn't be late.

"C'mon, Barb, we're in Italy!" I'd groan. "Why do I have to eat a healthy salad every day and then go for a walk? Just once I'd like to take a nap after lunch!" I knew my motion would be summarily dismissed as irrelevant.

"You can sleep when you're dead," Barbara replied dryly, lacing up her tennis shoes. "Just think of all the good exercise we're getting."

Invariably, I would give in. Barbara was right. The exercise was good for us, and besides, there was nothing else to do. Privately, I would bitch and moan, resenting the fact that the most important part of my day included walking with Barbara, whose energetic pace put my less-than-cooperative attitude to shame.

As we walked, I daydreamed of the life I lost in exchange for the one I now had.

...Back in the day, my PT was finished by 0700. I was strong as an ox, I felt great, and I was confident. Every day I'd do my part for the war effort—and I was earning big bucks, thank you very much. Now look at me: I'm miserable, I don't have the energy I used to, and the only thing on my schedule each day is to go for a walk after lunch. Whiskey, Tango...

The first few months after leaving Afghanistan were dark times for me. I should have been satisfied; life wasn't so bad. It was actually quite good, but the problem was that I was feeling sorry for myself and receiving no quarter from Barbara. She wouldn't go there; she was struggling with her own demons. She missed the life she had in Bahrain, the freedom of living in a 5,000-square-foot villa, fully furnished with handmade carpets and all the eclectic trinkets we had acquired over the years. She missed the year-round warmth and, of course, Penelope, her Jeep, which we sold because the price of fuel in Italy is around eight dollars per gallon, and the cost of insurance for a sport utility vehicle is prohibitively expensive, over $2,000 per year.

With time to spare, we decided to do some traveling. My newfound calling as a man of leisure meant I was no longer restricted to limiting our vacations to two weeks. Our post-Afghanistan holiday program included a trip to the US for three weeks, to check on a business opportunity in Texas. Our goal was to open a small business, but around every corner an obstacle discouraged us from making a long-term commitment. We had the money, but we couldn't convince ourselves that spending a couple hundred thousand on a never before tested enterprise and buying a house in a town we'd never been to before was the right thing to do, so we returned to Italy, repacked our bags, and went on vacation.

Photo from author's collection.

Barbara and I spent a month in Egypt at our favorite resort on the Nile. In the middle of our vacation we ventured over to Jordan to visit the Roman ruins of Jerash. We also visited Petra, the ancient city that was carved out of the mountains. We floated on the Dead Sea and coated our bodies with rejuvenating mud that smelled of sulfur. Living each day without concerns, and not having to be anywhere at any particular time, was liberating, and yet, the prospect of resuming some form of productivity flashed in my subconscious like a low battery signal on a cell phone.

Shortly after returning, I was offered a job from an entrepreneur and colleague who owned a UK-based company with contracts in Afghanistan. The position entailed doing some operations management in Kabul, with some preliminary training at the corporate offices in London. On my first day at work, I was surprised to learn that my employer hadn't taken the time to assign me with any tasks, or provide me with a place to work: no desk, nor even a chair to sit in. Left to my own devices, I found a place to sit and worked on the book you've been reading. After several weeks in London, it became apparent that I wouldn't be returning to Afghanistan anytime soon. I tried unsuccessfully to contact the entrepreneur, but he was unavailable. Most people might have been satisfied receiving a handsome annual salary and a free corporate apartment for doing nothing each day, but I'm a bit of an oddball; I resigned and returned to Italy to continue my sabbatical.

No matter how I tried, I couldn't get the thought of Afghanistan out of my head. I missed working with the troops, collaborating with others in support of multimillion-dollar projects, and sharing meals at the DFAC with my buddies. I felt bored much of the time in the real world, and the boredom was accompanied by crankiness. I was also feeling somewhat suffocated by the fact that Barbara and I were spending nearly every hour of every day together. I'm sure Barbara was feeling the same toward me, but since I was the cranky one she avoided the urge to exacerbate the situation further.

On our daily walks, Barbara would talk about how she wanted to restore the house and decorate the garden etc., for, like all good women who possess that nurturing quality that men appreciate, she had an interest in building her nest and turning it into a comfortable home. While describing the color of the parquet floor, or the pellet stove she wanted in the living room, I was usually preoccupied, trying to figure out how to maintain the quality of life we were accustomed to enjoying—without taking a job on the other side of the world, where I'd be alone, or subject to being shot at.

The US military is highly proficient at taking care of its service members' needs on and off the battlefield. Returning vets from the war zone are generally given whatever assistance they need to assimilate back into the real world. This might include taking some leave time, or attending training sessions to review procedures they need to resume a normal, healthy lifestyle. Similar programs existed within some of the larger companies that hired civilian contractors, but most of the contractors who returned home were left to fend for themselves.

I wasn't present to witness other contractors' homecomings, but I would wager that most of them returned to the reunions they'd experienced while on R&R—with one exception: this time, there would be no going back to Afghanistan. In some cases, the contractors were greeted with cheers; a welcome-home party was thrown, and life resumed as if nothing extraordinary had occurred. In most cases, however, there was probably less fanfare, if any at all. The contractor returned home, unpacked, sat around while the world sped by, and pondered what he or she should do next. If another job had been lined up, that was a plus. If not, the challenges of returning home were amplified. When left idle, the mind has a way of playing tricks on people.

Many contractors came home to family members who had become strangers. While working downrange, life had moved on without them. They were neither ignored nor forgotten intentionally; everyone was just busy living their own lives. Unless a spouse, partner, or some other conscientious observer took notice of the contractor's condition, then the burden of reconnecting with family members, friends, and the real world would fall on the shoulders of the returnee, who was understandably preoccupied with a myriad of other uncertainties, like what to do next.

By the end of 2013, thousands of civilian contractors had already begun repatriating back from whence they came. In many cases, extreme lapses in time had transpired while the breadwinner had been away. Within twenty-four months of my return from Afghanistan, most of the civilian contractor workforce was either redeploying to other jobs outside of Afghanistan, or reuniting with family and friends. After thirteen years of pursuing Al-Qaida and the Taliban, the military forces of the United States and NATO handed Afghanistan over to itself. For the contractors, that final exodus provided an opportunity to reflect on what had been a lengthy, exciting, challenging, and often stressful period. It was also a time to review what had been lost and gained.

In the loss column, there were those who didn't make it home. I knew several, and they will be in my thoughts every time I reflect on the hardships my colleagues and I endured. People experienced a variety of other losses as well. Many went through divorces or alienation from children and other family members, resulting from extended periods of separation. Regretfully, I happen to have quite a bit of knowledge on that subject. I don't have statistics, and I doubt any surveys were taken of contractors who returned from the battlefield, but I wouldn't be surprised if a segment of the contractor population had trouble readjusting after returning home. I'm not talking about anything as severe as a post-traumatic stress disorder (PTSD), but considering the number of contractors who served consecutive contracts, year after year, the possibility of a noncombatant contracting PTSD was not unlikely.

I struggled with trying to forget about Afghanistan for a number of years. I don't know why it was such a challenge for me. It wasn't a nice place; the living conditions weren't anything to write home about and people were shooting at us all the time. Perhaps, like prisoners who become institutionalized by their peculiar surroundings, year after year, we also became strangely accustomed to the world we lived in.

As we continue examining the loss column, I should note that both contractors and warfighters were aware of the fraud, waste, abuse, and infidelity that was rampant downrange. During activities that were intended to be honorable, and in support of serving the greater good, it was discouraging to see people ignore the moral values they were predisposed to honor while living at home.

Having witnessed the ugly side of war, idealists, good-natured souls, and even the crustiest veterans could leave the battlefield feeling disillusioned, disgusted, jaded, or betrayed. Some would look upon the war in Afghanistan as having been a total waste of money and the unnecessary killing of thousands. Others viewed it as another missed opportunity to accomplish something of global importance. If the purpose of going to war in Afghanistan was to eliminate Al-Qaida and dismantle the Taliban regime, then many would argue that we failed to do as much as we could have. As a result, our lack of commitment gave birth to a stronger and more savage threat, the likes of which have gained notoriety through acts of barbarism and tyranny throughout Iraq, Syria, France, and America. The Islamic State of Iraq and al Sham (ISIS) are well organized and unafraid of showing their strength in numbers. It appears to me, therefore, that the radical Islamic terrorists have yet to be dissuaded; they're bolder, more powerful, and perversely persistent.

I think it's fair to say that a large percentage of the people who served either lost or failed to ever gain compassion for the Afghan people, many of whom were either innocent bystanders or passive-aggressive participants who acted out of fear for their own safety. Lorenzo's unselfish and unconditional loyalty for the Afghan children warmed my heart, but I could never act with such unbiased benevolence. In some respects, Lorenzo was more human than most of us—which was a shame, but not in the sense that the rest of us had failed.

For when you consider how biased people's perceptions could be, especially when they were impacted by horrific events taking place around them, it's understandable how people might overlook the innocence of a child. I'm not saying such an oversight is justified; I'm simply explaining how people tend to lose perspective. An example of this can be illustrated by a recalling an episode in Herat, in which some colleagues and I witnessed an Italian Mangusta helicopter strafing a local village. I'm neither proud nor ashamed of the fact that we were cheering as the gunship put the smackdown on what was probably an enemy hideout—and there could have been civilian casualties involved, as well. Did we care? Not in the least. Did we express concern over the potential for collateral damage? Nope. That'll probably come off as seeming terribly insensitive to some, but you have to consider our point of view: as a result of the rain of fire delivered by the Italians, the rocket attacks we received each week subsided.

Fortunately, there were a number of benefits that could be taken into account. For starters, segments of the Afghan population enjoyed a surge of economic prosperity, resulting from the extended period of commerce; local businesses sprouted everywhere. One of the most popular local enterprises was to offer logistic services, which sold everything from building materials and construction equipment to automobiles and labor services. Communities sprouted along the highways between military bases. First aid and healthcare were provided to the locals by the coalition forces, and schools were built so children—who would have otherwise been denied an education—could learn to read and write.

As you might expect, a number of international and US companies profited from the war as well. *USA Today*'s March 2013 story "10 Companies Profiting the Most from War" reported that in 2011, the one hundred largest companies had sold $410 billion in arms and military services. Staggering amounts of money were spent on ships, aircraft, technology, and weapons systems that most contractors didn't even know existed. Granted, we saw the drones and jet fighters, with their laser-guided munitions and high-tech gadgetry, but the level of technology involved in those activities was above and beyond what most contractors were exposed to. Our field of view seemed to focus more on HESCOs and containerized housing modules. HESCO Bastion produced lightweight, easy-to-assemble blast-mitigating barriers that were about as common throughout Afghanistan as fish are to the sea. Remember one my favorite quotes: "War is hell, but it certainly makes for some great employment opportunities."

One of the more popular questions I was asked while serving in Afghanistan (and still today) was: How much did contractors earn while serving in a war zone? Salaries varied, depending on several factors, which included the contractor's skill set and the degree of danger that was present while they were performing their jobs. The American Professional Overseas Contractors, a group that works with the US military forces abroad, estimated that the average contractor in Afghanistan earned approximately $93,961 per year. Other sources claimed that the average daily wage was between $500 and $700, which pencils out to about $140K and $200K per year. Third country nationals (TCNs) earned less, which accounted for the large influx of TCNs who were hired by some of the larger defense contractors, such as KBR and FLUOR, toward the end of the war.

Every year that the war continued, the US government endeavored to pay less for the same level of service they received during previous years. As the government's defense budget shrank, contractor salaries were among the first to be impacted. By 2014, the NBA salaries (as we used to call them) paid during the initial stages of the war had all but disappeared. Today, contractors are earning even less for executing tasks that are still dangerous. Al-Qaida hasn't quit the fight, nor have the insurgents, whose dedication to maintaining Afghanistan's sovereignty has yet to be dissuaded.

There were intangible benefits as well. I'll always treasure the sense of pride I felt while serving in the military and then playing a supporting role as a contractor. I know I'm not alone in expressing these sentiments, there were literally tens of thousands of contractors in Afghanistan who had served in uniform at some time in their lives. Their ability to remain calm and execute complex tasks under incredibly stressful conditions was an inspiration to their colleagues. I would go even further by saying that the examples they set, probably saved lives.

After the war, I put pencil to paper and tallied up all the projects I had served on. The total value of the contracts I supported exceeded $750 million. As a builder from Southern California, I never imagined being involved in an endeavor so vast or significant as supporting the war effort. It's humbling to know that while being a part of something greater than myself, I accomplished far more than anything I could have achieved on my own.

Years after leaving Afghanistan, I can still remember everything as if it occurred only yesterday. I don't miss the challenges and the heartaches, but what I do miss is that feeling of satisfaction and pride. While serving as a contractor for what turned out to be an extended period of time (and one hell of an experience) I accomplished a great deal. More importantly, I learned even more about myself. Recording these events has been a cathartic process that has enabled me to reflect upon so many aspects of my life. I feel fortunate for all the blessings I've received yet sobered by the unfinished business that still remains.

I couldn't finish my story without paying one final tribute to the unsung heroes who deserve far more credit than they've received thus far, the other 100,000-plus contractors who served in Afghanistan. Many of us, in fact, are still in the fight, serving overseas. We're still toughing it out in some war zone, living somewhat of a Spartan existence away from home. *Contractoritis.*

If you're among that group, if you're like me, committed to staying downrange for the duration of an opportunity that offers (what I hope will be) a better return on my investment, then what are you waiting for? There's still work to be done.

Let's Roll!

Acknowledgments

Having finally completed this narrative I've come to learn that the process of recording memories, editing, and publishing a book requires a great deal of effort. My success would not have been possible without the assistance of family members, friends, and associates who participated in this project. The list of contributors includes but is not limited to the following people:

Rear Admiral Charles R. Kubic served thirty-five years in the Navy's civil engineering corps before retiring from the military in 2005. Several years later he co-wrote and published *Bridges to Baghdad*, his personal narrative that inspired me to record my story. I served under the admiral during my Gulf War II deployment with the FIRST Naval Construction Regiment at Pearl Harbor, Hawaii and we reconnected when I decided to put pen to paper and write about my escapades. My adventures pale in comparison to the story of the admiral's remarkable career, but he never hesitated whenever I reached out to him for assistance. Chuck's how-to tips and candid advice on self-publishing were very helpful and most appreciated. *Thank you, Admiral Kubic, and Go Seabees!*

Kim Foster was the first of two editors who worked with me on this project. She set the foundation upon which I was able to develop a template to achieve my objective: tell a story that pays tribute to the unsung heroes who served in support of the war on terror. Kim's patience and encouragement taught me to write down everything, and process it later. I think she'll be pleased by what came of our little project and feel proud to know that the discipline she taught me to employ as a writer became a tool that I use to problem solve my everyday challenges. *Good job, Kim—and thanks!*

Believing I had finished the book, I sent the manuscript out to be read by my sister Susan, and three colleagues with whom I spent time in the Land of Not Quite Right: Larry Currid, Kurt Smith, and Pete Melin. All four read the initial draft and provided honest commentary and detailed notes. Without their inputs I wouldn't have acquired the confidence needed to continue this project. To my delight, they all said that they liked the story, which inspired me to work harder and produce something even better; I hope they enjoyed the final version. *Thank you all for helping.* By the way, my sister Susan Natali (a published author herself) has written a pair of travel books about Italy. If you're thinking about a vacation in Italy and need some help with your itinerary, buy Susan's books (online) and have yourself a great time. *Buon viaggio!*

I need to offer my special thanks to Larry Currid and Lorenzo Mulero for their generous photo contributions. Like most readers, I enjoy seeing photos of what the author experienced. Larry and Lorenzo have gigabytes of jpeg files that were both inspiring and helpful. I trust that everyone enjoyed their contributions.

Tom Fritz has been a good friend for over 40 years. He's an incredibly gifted and successful artist who is best known for his hugely popular paintings of hot rods, motorcycles, and vintage cars. Tom's notable work includes commissioned paintings for Hollywood film promotions, Harley Davidson Motorcycles, and stamps for the US Post Office. Tom created the concept for the cover of this book, which was expanded upon and finalized by JuLee Brand of Kevin Anderson & Associates. I would like to extend my heartfelt thanks to Tom for his contribution to this project, and of course, his unconditional companionship—which I have enjoyed for the better part of my life. For a look at Tom's incredible work, visit fritzart.com on the Internet.

Dr. Jennifer Banash is a successful and published author. Jennifer served as my second editor and was responsible for inspiring me to take a number of honest and candid "leaps of faith" in order to help the readers connect with my story. Everything I wrote in this book actually happened, it's all true, but some of the content includes admonitions that I never imagined wanting to share. By sharing some of the more personal aspects of my life, the intent was to provide readers with insight into the world of struggles that war zone contractors routinely face. On a personal note, my hope is that by sharing stories about of the heartaches and challenges I experienced, perhaps others will be enlightened to pursue a path upon which their burdens might be eased as well. If I can do it, then so can you.

Jennifer is a contributor and associate of Kevin Anderson and Associates (KAA) of New York, a prestigious firm of literary and publishing professionals who provided many of the services I needed to publish this book. KAA's efforts well-exceeded my expectations with prompt, fair, and friendly service. *Thanks, Jennifer, Kevin, and JuLee for an awesome job!*

In keeping with the theme of every academy award winning actor/actress who appear surprised by the fact that they achieved what they set out to accomplish (and can't think of anything else intelligent to say) I want to thank my parents, Edward and Rosemary Cullen. You did a great job of raising me and I love you both.

Finally, I have to say thanks to the love of my life, Barbara, who remained patient and understanding while I spent years on the computer, head down, focusing my attention elsewhere. Barbara's inputs and honest appraisal of the manuscript helped me produce a final product that I became satisfied with, and for someone (like me) who is rarely satisfied with anything, that's quite an accomplishment. *Ti amo, Barb!*

The Author

Kevin Cullen was raised in Los Angeles, California. For the better part of the past fifteen years most of his time has been spent overseas supporting the US military. Kevin and his wife, Barbara, enjoy traveling, making new acquaintances while on holiday, and spending time with their family. Shortly after completing *Downrange for the Duration*, Kevin reached out to his children in hopes of reestablishing the bond they once shared. The results (for the most part) were positive.

If you enjoyed reading this book, or have a story that you would like to share for Kevin's next book, (featuring a compilation of tales told by other contractors) email the author at: DR4tDinfo@gmail.com

20452023R00129

Made in the USA
Lexington, KY
05 December 2018